The Crimson Book and Other Evangelical Sermons

DINSDALE T. YOUNG

BAKER BOOK HOUSE
Grand Rapids, Michigan

Reprinted 1974 by
Baker Book House Company

ISBN: 0-8010-9905-6

PHOTOLITHOPRINTED BY CUSHING - MALLOY, INC.
ANN ARBOR, MICHIGAN, UNITED STATES OF AMERICA
1974

DEDICATED TO

THE TREASURED MEMORY OF MY DEAR FATHER

WILLIAM YOUNG, M.D.

BEST OF FATHERS. BEST OF MEN

" Ye *are come* . . . to the spirits of just men made perfect."

PREFATORY NOTE.

THE kindly reception accorded to previous volumes, and the assurance that the Lord has worked with them, seems to invite the issue of this book.

It consists of sermons addressed to my own congregation in the course of my regular ministry. Perhaps it would be more accurately described as consisting of notes of more extended extemporaneous discourses.

The title " The Crimson Book " has been chosen not only because it is the theme of the first sermon, but because crimson is the evangelical colour, and each sermon is—it is hoped—evangelical or evangelistic in scope or spirit.

May a broad and affectionate evangelicalism increasingly inspire the pulpit and permeate the churches !

PREFATORY NOTE

If the enthroned Saviour shine upon these pages, neither reader nor writer will regret that they were written.

DINSDALE T. YOUNG.

1903.

CONTENTS

CONTENTS

CONTENTS

I

THE CRIMSON BOOK

" Moses . . . took the blood . . . and sprinkled . . . the Book."
HEB. ix. 19.

IT has been thought a thing incredible. But why? "According to the law, I may almost say, all things are cleansed with blood" (Heb. ix. 22, R.V.). If *all* things were cleansed by blood under the Mosaic legislation, why should "The Book" be omitted? "The Book" referred to is the ancient Bible, the roll in which the law of Sinai was inscribed. It is termed in Exodus "the Book of the Covenant." Some have doubted much as to this record of Moses sprinkling the Book with blood, because it is not expressly told in Exodus (chap. xxiv.) where the sprinkling of the people and of the tabernacle and of "the vessel of the ministry" is narrated. But we need to remember that the books of Scripture are mutually supplemental. What is for any reason omitted by one historian may be recorded by

I

another. The historians of the Bible are inter-
dependent. And we here find a striking fact
which had escaped the pen of the writer of Exodus
preserved for us by the author of the Epistle to
the Hebrews, one who, let him be who he may,
was deeply instructed in the history of the Mosaic
economy.

We do not know why the sprinkling of the
Book by Moses is unreported in Exodus ; but even
if it had been unreported also by the historian
of this epistle, most of us would be likely to
concur with the statement of Delitzsch, "That
Moses actually did sprinkle the Book of the
Covenant with the sacrificial blood might be
inferred by analogy."

The Revised Version lends emphasis to the
fact, for it reads, "Moses . . . took the blood . . .
and sprinkled . . . the Book *itself.*"

It was a strangely significant act. Nor can it,
if we ponder it, be deemed superfluous. Weird,
and not devoid of tragic suggestion, is the ritual-
istic deed. And it is a symbolic rite of deep
and abiding meaning. When Moses sprinkled
the Book with blood, his priestly achievement was
an acted parable. This sprinkling of the olden
Bible is an action not only picturesque, but of
eternal import. What if it can be shown that

for evermore the Bible is a blood-besprinkled
revelation? Let us see if it be not true that the
Bible is a Crimson Book.

I. "THE BOOK" IS AN ETERNAL SUBJECT OF
BLOOD-SPRINKLING.

We have already described "the Book" here
alluded to as the ancient Bible. It was the word
of God, indited by His servant, for Israel in the
wilderness.

Then there has always been a Bible in the
Church. The Church in the desert had its
revelation. How ancient a volume is the Bible!
Our religion is a book-religion in a very obvious
sense. All great religions are book-religions.
They would soon cease if "the Book" ceased. It
is easy to depreciate "the Book"; but without it,
alike in Mosaic and in Christian times, religion
would have but slight guarantee of permanence.

How much nobler a "Book" is ours than the
Book that Moses had! Woe be to us if we under-
value it, depreciate it, or neglect it! Compare
the Mosaic Bible with the Christian Bible, and
it is "as moonlight unto sunlight, or as water
unto wine." Nay, it is as the cold grey dawn to
the blazing meridian. Yet thank God for "the
Book" that Moses sprinkled. There can be no

meridian without the preparatory dawn. The Bible of ancient Israel is the foundation of the Christian Bible. In "the Book" that lay on the altar of Moses the present-day Bible was latent. Do not contemn the rude acorn that secretes a potential forest.

Let us make as much of our Bible as Moses and Israel made of theirs. They prized their "Book" right dearly. It was their fountain-light. They revelled in their Crimson Book. A sorry spectacle we shall be at the Great White Throne if ancient Israel transpire to have made more of their imperfect Bible than we of our far nobler Book. Make more and more of the Bible. Let your appeal be increasingly to its statutes. When your faith fails or flags, lay to heart the fine words of Dr. Fairbairn : " For the Christian spirit there is no secret of rejuvenescence like a bath in the original sources."

"Moses . . . took . . . blood . . . and sprinkled . . . the Book."

1. *Moses is nothing without " the Book."* Even Moses, with whom God spake face to face, is not independent of his Bible. Not even he can serve the Church without a Bible. Not even he can be a substitute for the record of divine revelation.

We need to lay that lesson to heart in these days. No personality, however resplendently spiritual, can count as sufficient apart from the word of God. Christ Jesus Himself came not without a constant appeal to the Bible. It has been pointed out that Christ retained the word "scribes" as a designation of New Testament preachers. That is a most significant fact.

The Bible is our supreme appeal—is, and must ever be. There has been an ominous disposition of late to substitute "Moses" for "the Book"— to accept the Christ and His apostles, ancient and modern, without their "Book." It is a dangerous and destructive tendency. To disparage the Bible in the supposed interest of the glory of Christ is the maddest of all disparagements. Let no modern "Moses" fail to make "the Book" his constant, unique, and infallible standard of appeal in things spiritual. Let "the Book" be the conspicuous feature of the Christian sanctuary. What St. Cyril of Jerusalem said to his catechumens every Christian teacher should unfalteringly say to his people: "Do not believe me simply, unless you receive the proof of what I say from Holy Scripture."

"Moses . . . took . . . blood . . . and sprinkled . . . the Book."

2. *Ceremonialism is nothing without " the Book."*
Moses had an elaborate ritual. Associated with
that "altar under the hill" was a strange series
of rites. Everything and everyone was crimsoned
with typical blood. There was " an altar," and there
were ministrants and sacrifices. But "the Book"
was the central item. Out of "the Book" Moses
read unto the people. All the ceremonialism was
regulated by and subordinated to "the Book."
This, again, is a fact of exhortative significance for
us in these Christian times. Still, Chillingworth's
dictum, rightly interpreted, is distinctly true : "The
Bible, and the Bible alone, is the religion of
Protestants." Even Protestants are liable to
forget that glorious fact. The "altar," and the
ministry, and the "water and scarlet wool and
hyssop" may easily throw "the Book" into the
shade. Oh, watch against that subtle and infinite
peril ! Let the Bible be prominent in *our worship*—
the one basis of pulpit-teaching, the one source
of Church-instruction ! Not the noblest literature
must rival the Book of God in our Churches. Let
the Bible be honoured in *our lives*. We may so
live, as the Master did, that we shall recall men
to the Scriptures. A godly life is a popular
commentary on the Bible. Men will believe the
Scriptures when we live them.

Oh, prize " the Book "! Be loyal to its precepts. When Moses read the Book " in the audience of all the people," the awed and instructed people cried with holy unanimity, " All that the Lord hath said will we do, and be obedient." Shall not we, as we hear and read the Book, make similar avowal?

" Search the Scriptures." Dr. Chalmers once prayed in his divinity class that he and his students might study Scripture until the day-star arose in their hearts. We do well fervently and perpetually to re-echo that glorious prayer.

II. IT IS AN ETERNAL NECESSITY THAT " THE BOOK " BE BLOOD-BESPRINKLED.

When Moses sprinkled the aforetime Bible with blood, it was far from an unmeaning ritualism. In verse 22 we read that according to the law " without shedding of blood there is no remission." The word translated " shedding " is very vivid, and really means " outpouring." Voluminous blood was the condition of remission in the Mosaic era. That blood was symbolic and prophetic. " Forward it cast a faithful look " to the atoning sacrifice of the Incarnate Saviour. If that is not its explanation, we know of no adequate explanation. If the ancient leviticalism does not foreshadow the eternal evangelicalism, then it is all but meaningless.

When Moses sprinkled his Bible with blood, he proclaimed an eternal necessity. The Bible must evermore be blood-besprinkled. Only a Crimson Book can meet our heartmost needs. And the Christian Bible is all over, and through and through, sprinkled with blood. Yes, with "the Blood of Jesus Christ," which Paul did not scruple to call the Blood of God. Our contention is that this is an eternal necessity, and we will presently endeavour to justify this contention.

Meanwhile, who can deny that the Bible is blood-besprinkled? We do not like that word "blood." "The red word," one of our novelists calls it. But the very word runs through the Bible. And the doctrine of the atoning virtue of Christ's blood is the great characterization of Scripture. It is prophesied in the Old Testament, and in the New Testament revealed. The whole book is crimson with redemption. I cannot pretend to be able to explain the mystery of the fact, but assured fact it is. This we know, that it represents an eternal necessity. We propose to inquire into this necessity. Why is "the Book" essentially blood-besprinkled? Why this Crimson Book?

1. *The blood guarantees the veracity of the Book.*
This, it seems to me, was the earliest signification
of the act of Moses.   He sprinkled the Book
with blood as a sign of the truth of the contents
of the Book.   The blood was God's endorsement
of the Book.   It was God's ensanguined auto-
graph.   Very full of meaning is the title of the
Book of Moses.   It was called (in Exodus) "the
Book of the Covenant."   In the verse which
follows my text, we are told that when Moses
sprinkled the Book he said, "This is the blood
of the covenant which God hath commanded
to you-ward" (R.V.).   The blood ratified the
covenant contained in the Book.   The blood is
the blood of a sacrifice God has enjoined and
accepted, and when it stains the Book the people
know that all that the Book saith is true.

It is a fact which portends much, too, that
we are told in the very verse from which I
take my text that the blood was sprinkled on
the Book "when every commandment had been
spoken by Moses unto all the people, according
to the law."   He has just read the Book of God
to the thrilled multitude, and then he sprinkles
upon it the sacrificial blood, and that blood
attests the inviolable veracity of the Book.   As
it is a Book of the Covenant, it is endorsed by

blood ; and as it is a statute-book, it is authorized by blood. God chooses to make "the blood" His sign of fidelity.

Brethren, these things are a parable. *Our* Bible is sprinkled with the divine Redeemer's blood. Let sneerers dub the book as gory; we glory in its ruby redness. To us the blood-besprinkledness of the Bible is the guarantee of its everlasting veracity.

How know we whether we can safely accept its words? The blood of Jesus streaks its every page. The atonement which it records abundantly endorses it. " He that spared not His own Son, but freely delivered Him up for us all "—He it is who speaks the revelations of the Bible. The Book is sealed with Jesus' blood. Why may I accept its precepts? Because the God who gave them provided for me an atoning sacrifice. Why should I obey its admonitions? Because the blood of the Saviour attests them true. Why should I dread its threatenings? Because to disobey Him who has given His Son for me must be criminality of acutest degree. Why may I believe its precious promises? Because I surely cannot doubt the goodness and fidelity of a God who has given me a Book red with the record of redemption. If He gave

His Son, He will freely give us all things. A blood-besprinkled Bible is a Bible whose veracity is established.

2. *"The blood" consecrates the Book.* When Moses sprinkled the Book with the blood of accepted sacrifice, he thereby made the Book sacred in the people's eyes. True, being a record of God's words, it was essentially sacred ; but "the blood " clothed it with superlative sanctity—a sanctity so singularly expressed that none could fail to realize it.

We speak to-day of " the *holy* Bible." The Scriptures themselves speak of themselves as " the *sacred* writings " (R.V.). Wherein is their holiness or sacredness? Many great answers might be given, but I submit that this is the greatest,— The Book is blood-sprinkled! It is throughout incarnadined with Jesus' blood. Ah! that gives it its awful consecration. This evokes our utmost reverence for the Book. We can never submit to its being classed as an ordinary book. It has no rival. In these days of hypercriticisms we need to revert to the old-fashioned awe of the Bible. See that ye reverence the Book. Tremble at it. You are not its judge. It is your judge, both now and at the last day. The Book of redemption is indeed a sacred Book.

When I see the blood of its Author sprinkled over it, I bow before the holy Bible.

3. "*The blood*" *cleanses the Book from defilement.* When we read that Moses sprinkled the Book with blood, we marvelled, and we said, "Did the Book need cleansing?" And, in a sense, it did. What! God's Book needed cleansing? Yes. For it had come into contact with sinful man, and man leaves injurious traces even upon a divine Book. Moreover, though the Book was inspired of God, it was written by man. "*Moses* wrote all the words of the Lord." So blood must be sprinkled upon the Book, as a sign that human authorship did not impair the validity of the records. Even the ancient Bible needed the influence of atonement, that it might be, as Delitzsch put it, "the immaculate monument of an abiding covenant." All defilement is cleansed from the Bible by the blood of Jesus which sprinkles it. Thank God, it is an undefiled book! No trace of stain is on its gleaming pages. Assuredly it is a purged Book. And it is the precious blood of Christ which cleanses it. We may well say to all depreciators of the holy Book, "What God hath cleansed call not thou common."

4. "*The blood*" *gives authority to the Book.* This is the special point referred to in the text. Blood

was the sign of authority. Blood lent force to all sacred things. And the blood gave the ancient Bible its power. The dispensations are called in the context testaments and covenants. The Book was in one aspect the record of a testament or will. Now, "a testament is of force where there hath been death : for doth it ever avail while he that made it liveth?" (ver. 17, R.V.). Can I be sure that the testament or will inscribed in the Scriptures is " of force "? Does it "avail"? Yes ; it is exceedingly abundantly effectual. But how can we be sure of this? The blood of the divine Testator sprinkles the Scriptures. This assures me " there hath been death," and I may joyfully accept the gracious and glorious provisions of the testament.

In another aspect the Bible is the record of a covenant. When Moses sprinkled the Book with blood, he exclaimed, " This is the blood of the covenant which God commanded to you-ward " (ver. 20, R.V.). The blood-sprinkling ratifies the covenant. How know I that I may depend upon the covenant which in this Book is described? The blood which stains its pages assures me.

We hear much in these times concerning the authority of the Bible. I contend that it is the atoning sacrifice which it proclaims that gives it its authority. The supreme message of Scripture is the atonement of Christ, and that atonement lends indisputable authority to the Book. I cannot disbelieve the testament, for the blood of the Testator reddens the writing. I cannot discredit the covenant, for the Maker of the covenant endorses it with His precious blood. I cannot but accept the authority of the Bible when I see it blood-besprinkled. Dare we reject a revelation invested with authority so pathetic and absolute ? A Book so crimsoned is a Book at all costs to be obeyed. The blood of Jesus the Son of God is the authority of Holy 'Scripture.

5. *" The blood" proclaims pardon as the message of the Book.* Thank God that for ever the holy Book is blood-besprinkled ! Were it otherwise, the Book would be an indictment. Without the message of " the blood of God " shed for our salvation the Bible would be a Book of doom. Sprinkled with that holy blood, it is the Book of salvation. When Moses sprinkled the Book and the tabernacle and the people, he thereby declared that there was pardon for the penitent sinner.

Still and evermore the Bible is crimson with blood, even with the blood of Jesus, and therefore its transcendent message is pardon. Pardon every soul may have, for Christ's blood was shed for all men. Whatever else the Atonement means, it means a message of forgiveness. We cannot hope to understand *how* the Atonement secures pardon. Redemption is an eternal mystery. Not even the clear-visioned angels can discern its infinite depths. We accept the sacrifice we cannot understand. Faith glories over knowledge. As Mr. A. J. Balfour says of the Atonement, it is "a mystery which, unless it were too full for our intellectual comprehension, would surely be too narrow for our spiritual needs."

O ye who mourn your sin, God's Book is eloquent of pardon. The blood of Jesus is sprinkled on its every page. Sin is the most dreadful fact of life. Dr. Pusey avows that "the sun never sets on sin." It is a shameful fact. And the sun never sets on *our* sin, *my* sin! Oh! where is rest of conscience to be found? How shall my sin cease to haunt me? Behold the message of the Book! Christ's blood sprinkles it, and may sprinkle me. I trust that blood, and will trust it, nor shall any other trust intrude upon my guilty soul. Too often I have been (as Baxter phrases it) "a disesteemer of Thy blood"; but henceforth, by Thy grace, O God of pardons, I will accept the message of Thy Crimson Book!

6. "*The blood*" *publishes cleansing as the purpose of the Book.* It is a suggestive comment made by the writer of the epistle before us, that by the law all things are "*cleansed* with blood" (ver. 22, R.V.). Yes; the sprinkling of the blood was symbolic of cleansing. The blood dashed on the holy Book is a declaration that through sacrifice there is cleansing. God would purify everything, and everything finds its purification in the blood of Jesus: that is the deep, far-reaching lesson of the sprinkled blood; that is the loftiest lesson of the Crimson Book.

My friends, this is the only gospel of cleansing. Sinners have no other hope. A simple faith in Christ's atoning blood can alone cleanse our natures. Holiness, in the New Testament sense of the term, is achieved only by "the blood of sprinkling." A whole-hearted reliance on the Saviour's sacrifice is the sole secret of ethical holiness. We are justified by faith in Jesus' blood, and by faith in that blood are we sanctified. When I see "the blood" sprinkling God's Book, I know that there is a sure hope of cleansing. You have heard the ofttold story of the Romanist who had never read his Bible for himself, and realized the free salvation it proclaims. " Wife," he exclaimed, " if this Book is true, we are lost!" But as he read on, and the evangelical salvation was revealed, he cried in rapture, " Wife, if this Book is true, we are saved!" Blessed be God! if we accept this Book we are saved. Not only are we pardoned, but we are cleansed from all sin by the blood most precious which sprinkles its divine pages. Oh! trust this holy blood, and thou shalt be holy too. Thou shalt fight thy good fight, and be more than conqueror, " because of the blood of the Lamb."

Moses sprinkled "all the people." The Crimson Book cannot save us unless we ourselves be sprinkled. The blood revealed in the scripture must be applied to our nature. Are *we* sprinkled with the Redeemer's blood? Is all our everlasting hope in the blood of the Lamb? Let our one all-sufficient plea be this: " Thy blood was shed for me."

The recreant Jews imprecated Christ's blood upon themselves and their children. Be our *prayer* this: " His blood be upon us, and upon our children."

II

CHRIST COMING BY WATER AND BLOOD

"This is He that came by water and blood, even Jesus Christ; not by water only, but by water and blood."—I JOHN v. 6.

SUCH is John's portrayal of the Saviour. It is true alike of the historical Jesus and of the mystical Christ. Surely only the mystical John was capable of so sublime a conception.

The apostle has just been speaking of the object of Christian faith. He declares that faith is the secret of overcoming "the world"—men and things considered as apart from God and hostile to God. But faith in whom? In "the Son of God." And how did He reveal Himself? My text is the magnificent response: "This is He that came by water and blood, even Jesus Christ; not by water only, but by water and blood."

Let me call your attention, first, to certain expository matters essential to a comprehension of this evangelical testimony.

"This is He that *came*." That word "came" has here a noteworthy meaning, as indeed it frequently has when used of Christ in the New Testament. It has been described as a "technical" term. Our Lord is spoken of as "He that cometh," and as "the prophet that cometh." The coming referred to is "technical." The reference is not merely to His incarnation or His advent, but to His self-revelation. He manifested His nature and character and work. He flashed His splendour upon the dark universe. That is the scope of the word "came" as John uses it here. He declares that Jesus Christ manifested Himself "by water and blood." The water and blood were the media of His self-revelation. The word "by" carries that idea. It is as if John said, "This is He that evidenced His nature, character, and work in the elements of water and blood."

Notice, also, that the full name "Jesus Christ" is deeply significant. The names of our Lord are never used haphazardly in Scripture. Jesus is the human name : Christ the official designation. If either be used separately, the one special aspect of His nature is emphasized. When both are associated, the two aspects are declared. Here the complete name indicates the dual nature of the Saviour.

What is the reference of the terms "water and blood"? It is evidently very specific. This is clearly seen in the rendering of the R.V.: "Not with *the* water only, but with *the* water and with *the* blood." The idea is that He came with these as the instrumentalities by which His work is to be accomplished. Water and blood were the criteria of His manifestation and the methods of His ministry.

Now what, I ask, is the definite historical reference? I regard it as threefold.

(*a*) Jesus Christ manifested Himself by water and blood in His baptism and in His crucifixion. He came by water. He was revealed and revealed Himself in that acted parable in Jordan, when, as the fulfiller of all righteousness, He emerged from the river glistering with the baptismal drops, and from the opened heavens the voice rang out, "This is My beloved Son, in whom I am well pleased."

He came by blood. See Him on yonder cross Hear Him as, wounded and bleeding, He cries, "It is accomplished." He revealed Himself in that surrendered life.

(*b*) The reference of the text is also undoubtedly to the pathetic and tragic episode of which John, in his gospel, is the only narrator. A soldier with a spear pierced His side, and forthwith there came out blood and water. It was a heart-moving parable. So Christ's earthly ministry is bounded, at its start and at its close, by a parabolic incident.

(c) I believe a third reference of these words is sacramental. Jesus Christ came by "the water and the blood" in the sense that He instituted the two rites of Christian Baptism and the Lord's Supper. In these He revealed Himself even as He did in His personal baptism and crucifixion, and in the piercing of His side.

He came by water. He instituted water-baptism, and manifests Himself in it. I will not now discuss modes of baptism, nor the stage of life at which the rite should be obeyed. But I will assert that it seems to me to be a scriptural obligation that all Christians should undergo the rite. If any have not been baptized in infancy, and thus dedicated to Christ vicariously, let them hasten to dedicate themselves personally by adult baptism. For still and evermore Jesus Christ comes by "the water."

He also came by "the blood," in the sense that He instituted the ordinance of the Lord's Supper. I prefer the term "ordinance" to "sacrament," as the one is scriptural and the other is not. Two elements are sanctified in the Lord's Supper, but John names only "the blood." It would be inappropriate here to name the bread, as it would mar the rhythm of the poet's symbolism. Christ revealed Himself in "the blood" which, mystically speaking, is discerned in "the cup" of the holy ceremony. And still He reveals Himself thus. Verily now and evermore He comes by "the blood."

Such, as I conceive, is the reference of these terms "the water and the blood."

Now, let us, as the Holy Spirit shall enlighten, seek to ascertain what are the eternal principles here inculcated : " This is He that came by water and blood, even Jesus Christ ; not with the water only, but with the water and with the blood."

I. CHRIST COMES WITH RIGHTEOUSNESS AND WITH REDEMPTION.

" The water " signifies righteousness, whether the reference be to Christ's baptism or to the pierced side or to Christian baptism. Christ came to reveal righteousness and to impart it to men. But observe John's emphatic denial that Christ came only with righteousness : " Not with the water *only*, but with the water and with *the blood*." Why this emphasis on the coming with blood? Surely because some of those to whom John writes needed the stringent reminder. There were those who saw the Christ in the water, but not in the blood. There were those who denied that the Deity dwelt in Jesus when He shed His blood on Calvary. They believed in a divine righteousness, but not in a divine redemption.

How the Bible gives a light to every age! How the conditions of to-day are represented in those of bygone times! Many stand exactly where those stood to whom John wrote, and they need the exact reminder John gives.

There are those who to-day accept the Christ who came with the water, but rejected the Christ who came with the blood.

Still, we need to cry, " Not with the water only, but with the water and with the blood."

Unquestionably Christ came with water. He brings to men a noble quality of righteousness, a splendid morality, an ineffable idea of conduct.

Let no Christian depreciate morality. Do not speak of it as " mere " morality. True, the word only signifies an attitude or manner, but a right moral attitude or manner is of great price. Without good honest morality no creed or profession is of the slightest worth. Christ came with water. He taught and lived an incomparable righteousness. He thus revealed Himself. And such a righteousness He imparts to all who will receive it. He cleanses by His Spirit the soul that trusts Him. He makes moral men. The most impressive testimony to the moral ideal of Christ is that not even His truest followers ever perfectly attain it. There never flowed such a river of God "clear as crystal" as that which Christ comes by.

But He came also "with the blood." Christ brings redemption as well as righteousness. That is what many are in danger of forgetting in these days. Still, we need the inspired disclaimer, "Not with the water only."

The evangelical position is that Christ could not come with water if He did not come with blood. Redemption must precede righteousness. Atonement is essential to morality. Ancient guilt must be effaced before new righteousness can be attained. My yesterdays must be forgiven before my to-morrows can be sanctified. I believe with all my heart the sentiment of the evangelical hymn:

> The water cannot cleanse,
> Before the blood we feel,
> To purge the guilt of all our sins,
> And our forgiveness seal.

There is great peril in the insistence which some make upon the example of Christ. Christ's example cannot *save* men. That radiant example of holiness never yet saved a soul of man. No noble example ever had saving power. Beware, therefore, of a one-sided asking of the question, "What would Jesus do?" Acceptance with God is not in the answer of that grand inquiry. Sinners need redemption. The condemnation of their sins must be removed. This Jesus Christ effects: "He bore our sins in His own body on the tree." He came with the blood. He brings us plenteous redemption.

St. John, in recording the piercing of Christ's side, mentions the blood first; and in my text he puts sovereign emphasis upon the blood. There the emphasis should ever abide. Christ's redemption is causative of Christ's righteousness. It supplies the only adequate *motive*. How to find a sufficiently potent motive for morality has always been *the* problem of ethics. Christ solves the problem. He comes with water and with blood. By His redemption He gives a mighty motive for His righteousness. "He gave Himself for me" is the motive that has created more splendid morality than aught else beside. Redemption is not only an adequate motive, it is a *power* which infallibly produces morality. Trusting that precious blood, we are cleansed by that living water.

The atonement of Christ is the only force by which righteousness can be realized. Christ came with the water and with the blood—with righteousness and with redemption.

So in their degree must Christians come. Though in a vastly lesser sense, these words should be true of every follower of the Christ : " This is He that came by water and blood ; not with the water only, but with the water and with the blood." The world should be able to say this of the Church.

We must present a noble righteousness to the sons of men. We must do everything that "becometh us to fulfil all righteousness." We must experience the cleansing of the purifying stream which God promises to the believing soul. We must come by water. Oh the blessedness of practical righteousness ! Oh the peace and joy that spring from keeping God's commandments ! Oh the rapture of the righteousness the Holy Spirit imparts ! Dora Greenwell says, "Obedience is a direct means of grace." And so it is. What spiritual tranquillity and strength, and what fellowship with God, we have when we do the

Commandments. Brethren, seek moral perfectness. There is an apologetical value in Christian
morality. The world will accept our theology
when it witnesses our righteousness. We must
come by water.

But we must also come "with the blood." We
must bear testimony to the Christian redemption
in word and deed. We must make it manifest
that "the blood" is all our trust, and that we do
not trust it in vain. "Not with the water only"
must the modern Church come. Our character
and work must be a treatise on the Atonement.

II. CHRIST COMES WITH RITUAL AND WITH
SACRIFICE.

"The water" stands for the ritual, and "the
blood" for the sacrificial. When the Saviour
was baptized in Jordan, He came by water :
He sanctioned ritual. When he died on the
cross, He came by blood : He illustrated the
sacrificial.

Still He so comes by His Spirit and in His
Church. He reveals Himself in ritual. But "not
with the water only," more powerfully far by
sacrifice.

We are all ritualists. Christ was a ritualist.
It is all but imperative that faith must fix itself

to form. We speak of " the ritualists," often forgetting that ritualism is but a question of degree.
In our judgment " the ritualists " cultivate an
inordinate degree of ritual. But always let us
remember the rights of the individual conscience.
One man needs a simple ritual, another needs
elaborate ritual. Let each have freedom to
worship God in his own way. Ritual, however,
we all must have. The Society of Friends are
ritualists. Their simple service is a ritual.
Puritan worship has its ritual. And we may be
rank formalists with the simplest form of worship.
What are you making of your ritual? You—a
Puritan, perchance!—make much of your particular
order and form ; but what are you getting out of it ?
Do you truly worship? With a bald ritual our
heart may be far from God. Come " with the
water" as the Master did. Manifest Christ as
you observe the ritual of Christianity.

We too, though it must be in a far meaner
sense, must come " by blood." Christ came " not
with the water only." He shed His blood for
men. He delivered up His life for the world.
That blood must be our example as well as our
trust. But is it ? Christians must be sacrificial,
or their ritualism will avail them little. Sacrificial Christianity is supernatural Christianity. The

Church of the future must come with blood. Paul said, with startling boldness, that he filled up that which is behind of the afflictions of Christ. Few of us dare make such a claim. At the first assembly of Anglican bishops an American brother preached on that text. Witty Bishop Wilberforce dreaded the publication of the sermon, lest the bishops should be exposed to ridicule. He saw the incongruity of such a text. So did Archbishop Tait, who said in his diary that the festivities of the episcopal week did not look like afflictions. No; rarely do any of Christ's ministers come by "blood"! Do you, my Christian reader? You often dwell at "Ænon near to Salim, for there is much water there"; but do you ever pitch a crimson tent on Calvary? We ought to lay down our lives for the brethren, said John, because Christ laid down His life for us. But are we doing it? Oh, let us cultivate the spirit of sacrifice! Let us come by blood. Thank God, many a Christian is so doing. Dr. A. J. Gordon said of one of his enterprises, " So far the effort has not paid financially; but, what is far better, it has cost." Yes; it is always far better when a thing costs us than when it pays! "Blood" is ever precious. By sacrifice Abel yet speaketh. And the testimony of a Christian who comes "not with water only, but with blood," will sound on with everlasting eloquence.

III. CHRIST COMES NOT WITH PURE SPIRITU-ALITY, BUT WITH ORDINANCES.

He comes by water and blood. He introduced the ordinances in which water and blood are respective symbols. The human soul is incapable of appreciating pure spirituality. If there were here and there a rare soul who attained to that height, such exceptions would but prove the rule. The Incarnation is a protest against absolute spirituality. Man can only come at the spiritual by the natural.

The Saviour manifests Himself in His own appointed ordinances. He does not limit Himself to Baptism or the Lord's Supper, or to any particular ordinance. He comes in all sorts of ordinances. But the point to be noted is, that ordinances are His means of manifestation. We cannot do without "*means* of grace." We may lose the grace in neglecting the means. Are they obligatory? Let me answer in Bishop Gore's admirable words: "They are obligatory as food is obligatory."

Let us be loyal to the Christian ordinances. Edward Irving described preaching as "the royal ordinance." So it is. I believe it stands above all others. It is the highest expression of worship. "Despise not prophesyings" is peculiarly an admonition for this age, when exaggerated ritual on the one hand and shallow evangelism on the other hand are whittling down the significance of that royal ordinance of preaching.

But why be eclectic regarding ordinances? There is profit in all, benediction in each. Jesus was loyal to ordinances whilst incarnate here: so let us be. He instituted ordinances: let us conform to His designs. Let us come by water and blood.

IV. CHRIST COMES WITH WONTED METHODS AND WITH UNIQUE METHODS.

"This is He that came by water and blood." Moses had come by water: the Church in the wilderness was baptized unto him in the cloud and in the sea. Aaron had come by blood: his priesthood was great in its sacrifices. But Christ came with water and blood. "Not with the water only," nor with the blood only, but with both. Christ's methods were complete: all who ever came before Him used incomplete methods. The completeness of Christ's mode is its uniqueness. But when Christ used a wonted method, how unique He made it! Who ever came by water as He did? He used accustomed symbolism in unaccustomed ways. Who ever came with blood as He did? He came with "*His own* blood." He was infinitely original in His methods.

So also in its degree must the Church come. We do well to accept and utilize methods venerable and approved. We may, by grace, get the old blessing out of the old methods.

But, again in our degree, like our Master we do well to adopt new modes of service. Adaptation in Christian work is but loyalty to Christ's example. We must come by all the accustomedness and all the uniqueness that are symbolized by water and by blood.

A great rubric for all Spirit filled Christian workers is, "Do as occasion shall serve thee."

V. CHRIST COMES NOT WITH TRANSIENT BUT WITH PERMANENT INSTRUMENTALITIES.

"The water" and "the blood" are not destined to become extinct forces. Whilst the world lasts they will effectually operate. Christ's righteousness and Christ's redemption abide for ever. Christ's ordinances shall obtain "till He come."

The Lord's are permanent elements. His gospel is "an eternal gospel."

Then it is our wisdom to be "stedfast, unmoveable." Make always and for ever the most of all "the water" signifies. If it represent righteousness, then there is righteousness nowhere but in the grace of Christ. If it represent ordinance or ritual, then let us be diligent in that which He has enjoined. And may God keep us firmly trusting in that which "the blood" represents. The blood of Jesus Christ is the eternal instrument of justification. If it avail not, or if it be rejected, "there remaineth no more sacrifice for sin."

Oh, cleave ye to it with purpose of heart! Be that precious blood thy soul's one hope.

Have we received Him who "came by water and blood, even Jesus Christ"? Do we firmly and gratefully believe that He came "not with the water only, but with the water and with the blood"? "This is He." Oh, accept him! "This is He." Oh, seek a fuller knowledge of Him, a deeper devotion to Him! "This is He." But how shall I realize this? I call you to contemplate the words which immediately ensue upon my text: "And it is the Spirit that beareth witness" —immediately or through ministries of grace— "because the Spirit is the truth"—and therefore His testimony can be unreservedly accepted.

Does the Spirit "bear witness" to your heart and to your intellect that "this is He that came by water and blood, even Jesus Christ; not with the water only, but with the water and with the blood"? Ask for that attesting Spirit, and you shall receive Him. Then your glad cry concerning the Son of God will be, "This is He." Go, tell the first man you meet, "This is He." Proclaim it everywhere, "This is He." Ring out the evangel, "This is He." Flash the gracious light upon the dark world, "This is He." And when that illuminating gospel has accomplished its work, "the whole world shall be lighted as Eden was of old."

III

THE SUPREME SUPERIORITY

"The excellency of the knowledge of Christ Jesus my Lord."
PHIL. iii. 8.

JOHN HOWE says that Paul here speaks "in a rapture." And assuredly he does. The knowledge of Christ Jesus thrills his soul with a quenchless enthusiasm. Such knowledge must be very wonderful. Let us spend a moment on its definition.

What is this knowledge of which Paul speaks so glowingly? I think we shall wander far before we find a more apt and adequate definition than that of Matthew Henry: he defines it as "a believing experimental acquaintance with Christ as Lord." A *believing* acquaintance! Not merely a theoretical or scientific knowledge, but a trustful apprehension. An *experimental* acquaintance! Not an intellectual assent divorced from deeds but a cognizance which expresses itself in deeds. A faith which transforms the character—such is

35

"the knowledge of Christ" of which Paul sings in enraptured strains.

We do well to be very clear about this at the beginning. It is no mere intellectual knowledge of Christ Jesus to which Paul attributes such excellency. An arid unethical knowledge of the Saviour has no excellency. A fiend of the pit boasted of such knowledge. He said, "Jesus I know." But he remained a fiend for all that. Hell has a Christology. Demons are orthodox. Yet such Christology and such orthodoxy do not transform the character ; in fact, its Christology makes hell more hellish, and their orthodoxy makes demons more demoniacal.

My friend, hast thou "a believing experimental acquaintance with Christ as Lord"? Then thou hast the excellency of knowledge! Oh, be sure no other knowledge can avail! Make no mistake as to the quality of thy knowledge of Christ. Be not content to know Him but as the demon knows Him. The only "knowledge of Christ Jesus" that is worth the name is that of which Paul speaks— the knowledge of faith. In the Bible faith and knowledge are almost interchangeable terms. Faith is the higher knowledge. Be ours such knowledge of Christ. It is to *this* knowledge and no other that Paul attributes an unique and

eternal "excellency." The word here rendered
"excellency" is a remarkable word, and has
evoked a variety of translations. It is a superlative term. Paul was great at superlatives. The
great majority of New Testament superlatives are
from his ecstatic pen. His ardent heart flowed
forth in ardent terminology when he spake of
Christ Jesus his Lord. How extravagant, un-
measured, "enthusiastic" appears Paul's vocabulary
to this cold, formal age!

Dean Vaughan renders the original word "the
superiority." Dean Alford renders it "the super-
eminence." Bishop Moule reads it "the surpassingness." Associate these translations and what
a strong impression we have of Paul's estimate
of the knowledge of Christ! The excellency, the
superiority, the super-eminence, the surpassingness!
Truly it is in a rapture that Paul speaks. And
such spiritual perception will create such spiritual
rapture.

Paul's estimate of the knowledge of Christ Jesus
is the more wonderful when you realize the
antithesis he creates. He says a believing experimental acquaintance with Christ as Lord has an
"excellency":—above what? "*All things*" (v. 8).
It has a "super-eminence":—over what? "*All
things.*" It has a "surpassingness":—beyond

what? "*All things.*" What a bold, unqualified, and arresting claim! If Paul had declared that the knowledge of Christ Jesus had a supreme superiority over all knowledge it would have been a tremendous claim. But he goes further far than that: he claims that this "spirit sight" of Jesus is supreme above all things. Pile gold, silver, and precious stones Mont Blanc high: then pile mountains upon mountains: and the knowledge of Christ Jesus is super-eminent above all the resplendent heights. Accumulate all the precious things of life: all knowledge: all arts: all beauties: all loves: and the knowledge of Christ Jesus has a glory that infinitely excelleth. No marvel Paul elsewhere speaks of "the savour" of this knowledge. Verily it is the fairest and most fragrant flower that blooms.

Now wherein lies the excellency, the superiority, the super-eminence, the surpassingness of the knowledge of Christ Jesus? All good knowledge, and especially all knowledge of good personalities, is excellent, but what is the secret of the supreme superiority of this knowledge? Can it really be that "a believing experimental acquaintance with Christ as Lord" transcends the "all things" of the universe? Let us see if Paul's impassioned prediction can be justified.

I. THE KNOWLEDGE OF CHRIST JESUS AF-
FORDS A VIVID REVELATION OF GOD.

The problem of the ages is to know God.
Philip was humanity's spokesman when he cried,
"Lord, show us the Father." A sight of God!
For this man ever craves.

This passion is satisfied, satiated in Christ Jesus·
He is "God manifest." To get God manifested
has been the longing of generations. To have
God visible, palpable—for this the noblest spirits
of history have yearned. This was the craving
of the great pre-Christian seekers after God. In
Christ, and in Christ alone, is this inexorable
longing adequately met. His own great word
is, "He that hath seen Me hath seen the Father."
The Father is in character, purpose, spirit, what
Jesus Christ was. It is a great and wonderful
truth ; and elementary as it is, the Christianity
of the centuries has scarcely appreciated it.
Christ is a vivid revelation of God. Nowhere
else is a *vivid* revelation of the Father found.
I am not ignoring other and noble revelations
of God. We see God in Nature. His presence
is the splendid implication of all things. Creation
mirrors its Creator. We see God in man. He
shines in children's faces and speaks in the music

of children's voices. Have you not seen God
in your friend ? If you have not you have
missed the genius and grace of friendship. God
is everywhere, and all things are builded into
an holy temple of the Lord.

But no revelation of God is comparable for
vividness to the revelation of God in Christ.
As Godet finely puts it, " Jesus is God lived by
man." We see the authentic God in Christ
Jesus the Lord. Then indeed the knowledge
of Christ Jesus is invested with a superiority, a
super-eminence, a supassingness. What of the
" all things " is comparable to it ? for what else
can so vividly pourtray God ? When I have
" a believing experimental acquaintance with
Christ as Lord " I know God. I see the Father
in the Son. " All His Father in Him shone."
He is the effulgence of God's glory.

Oh what bliss thus to know Christ Jesus. Oh
the supreme superiority of this heart-knowledge !
The deepest longing of our noblest nature can
only be satisfied in Christ. We can only apprehend God in Christ. The only-begotten Son
and He alone, declares the Father.

Do you thirst for God ? Do you desire with
desire to see God ? Have you got as far as
the simple Christian believers of Labrador who

said to the Moravian missionaries: "We wish
to have such a longing for God as a child has
for its mother, or a man in the chase has for
the reindeer"?   Then I point you to Christ
Jesus.   To know Him is to be assured of God—
to see God.   Only in the Christ-fountain can
your immortal thirst be quenched.

The man who would have a great and absorbing
enthusiasm for God must study Him in Christ
and realize Him in Christ.   When we discern
what a gracious God He is in Christ, then we
cry with Tholuck, "I have but one passion: It
is He! It is He!"

The supreme thing of the universe is the knowledge of Christ Jesus which flashes a vivid vision
of God upon our awed and grateful ken.

II. THE KNOWLEDGE OF CHRIST JESUS
SECURES A GREAT EVANGELICAL SALVATION.

In this, again, we perceive the excellency,
the superiority, the surpassingness of such a
knowledge.   I said the problem of the ages is
to know God.   It is even more abundantly
this—"What must I do to be saved?"   The
dearest designation of Christ Jesus is "Saviour."
He solves this awful problem.   When I have "a
believing experimental acquaintance" with Him

I am evangelically saved. That is, my guilty
yesterdays are pardoned, and I am accepted of
God as His child. All knowledge has a certain
saving quality, but the knowledge of Christ
Jesus is the salvation of the guilty soul. Ecclesiastes says, "The excellency of knowledge is that
wisdom giveth life to them that have it."
(Eccles. vii. 12); but the supreme excellency
of the knowledge of Christ Jesus is that it
gives eternal life to them that have it. What
of "all things" can compete with it in this? Can
human learning? Can mere morality? Can
wealth? Nothing! Nothing! Then O the
supreme superiority of this saving knowledge!

The evangelical salvation which the knowledge
of Christ Jesus brings, is often set forth in the
Scriptures of truth. Let me adduce two examples.
The first is taken from the wondrous pages
of the Old Testament evangelist, Isaiah. In
his ruby-red chapter of redemption he declares,
"By His knowledge shall My righteous servant
justify many." That the reference of these words
and of the whole dramatic and pathetic chapter
is to the Saviour, is a fundamental belief of
evangelical Christians. Then what a word is this!
"By His knowledge (by knowing Him) shall
My righteous servant justify many"—pardon

them and set them in a new and happy relation
to God and His outraged law. O sublime and
wonderful experience! If I know Christ Jesus
with "a believing experimental acquaintance," all
my offences are pardoned, and I am reinstated in
the fatherly favour of my God. Can any other
power or influence procure me justification?
Assuredly none. Then how superior, super-
eminent, surpassing is the knowledge of Christ
Jesus.

Is this evangelical axiom sufficiently preached
to-day? Is this evangelical experience generally
enjoyed to-day? I wish I were more clear that it
is so. Brethren, only this believing knowledge of
Christ Jesus can put us right with our black bad
past: this alone can take our guilt away: this is
the one secret of a quiet conscience and a soul
flushed with a light above the brightness of the
sun. Acquaint thyself believingly with the redeeming Son of God. Cry, "I lay *my* sins on Jesus,"
and sure as you so do peace with God and with
yourself shall make your soul serene.

But I desire to be harmonized with my future
as well as with my past. Hear, then, another word
concerning the knowledge of Christ Jesus. In
His high-priestly prayer the Saviour says, "And
this is life eternal, that they might know Thee the

only true God and Jesus Christ whom Thou hast sent." A believing knowledge of God is the secret of eternal life, and such knowledge only comes by the knowledge of Jesus Christ. "This is life eternal:" life which is unlimited by time: life which mocks the death which seems to mock it: endless life: such a quality of life that it can never cease. Oh, how the problem of to-morrow distresses men as well as the problem of yesterday. What is there in the long future? Is there a long future? Beyond the grave—is it darkness unrelieved, or may it be marvellous light? The gnawing problem is solved in the knowledge of Christ Jesus, and in that alone. Let a man believingly acquaint himself with Christ Jesus, and the guilty past is blotted out, and the eternal future shines with unspeakable glory.

Such an evangelical salvation lies in the knowledge which in our text Paul so rapturously celebrates. No marvel he claims for that knowledge an excellency so ineffable. That which holds so great a salvation must indeed be the supreme superiority. Knowest thou Christ Jesus as thy personal Saviour? Canst thou join in Paul's song? There is no other hope for sinful man. I preach it absolutely and unreservedly as man's only gospel. When Julius Hare lay dying he bore this testimony: "All bridges that one builds through life fail at such a time as this, and nothing remains but the bridge of the Saviour." Oh, lay that impressive testimony, that irrefragable fact, to heart. Some of you are building golden bridges: beautiful bridges: bridges which are clever evidences of architectural originality. But none of them will sustain you in the hour and article of death. Only the bridge of the Saviour is adequate to that final stress. O ye bridge-builders, abandon your labour on that which cannot satisfy in the insatiable hour of death! Step now upon the bridge of the Saviour—that living bridge—and it will bear you, as it has borne myriads, across the gulf into the sweet fields which smile upon the other side.

III. THE KNOWLEDGE OF CHRIST JESUS PRESENTS A SUBLIME ETHICAL SALVATION.

The excellency, the super-eminence, the surpassingness of a believing experimental knowledge of Christ is grandly apparent in this. Christ Jesus is the supreme moral standard. Even atheists admit that in Christ moral perfection has its finest fruition. He ran the gamut of morality. He exhausted the possibilities of goodness. When I know Him I am, therefore, face to face with the noblest standard of morality. I see what the mountain-peak of ethics is. Christ's fulness of stature is the measure of moral perfectness. Never do we realize the loftiness of life's moral standard till we know Christ. Seeing Him we see what are the obligations and possibilities of the moral life. But the knowledge of Christ does far more than this. It imbues us with power to achieve the ideal set before us. This is where other moral and religious systems fail. They may present a shining standard of conduct, but they do not empower. They may illustrate their maxims by a noble example, but they fail to give an inward and adequate force whereby men may successfully emulate the example. Christianity offers to make moral ideals moral actualities. Christianity proposes to make the servant as his Lord. And it has done it in countless cases. How? By giving a believing experimental acquaintance with Christ, and this through the indwelling of the very Spirit of Christ. When men know Christ thus they become ever more and more conformed to Christ's image. They are changed from glory to glory even in greyest years.

What but the knowledge of Christ Jesus can give such an ethical salvation? Let this knowledge be judged by its ethical results.   Let Christianity stand or fall by the peerless morality it creates. It supplies a morality which is no mere outward pose but pervades the thoughts and intents of the heart.   It inbreathes a morality of motive.   It creates ethical propriety and beauty without by inspiring an ethical spirit within.   It transfigures the man's conduct by transfiguring the man himself.   Everywhere to-day the demand is for ethical perfection.   My fervent and ever-deepening conviction is that to know Christ is the only secret of such perfection.   To know Christ believingly is not alone to possess an evangelical salvation, but an ethical salvation too.   Christian evangelicalism vindicates itself by Christian ethics.   Christianity achieves sublime morality.

Begin your ethical culture at the right point. Do not essay to build from the top.   Commit yourself to Christ.   Know ye the Saviour.   He delivers from the guilt of sin.   But He gloriously delivers from the power of sin.   Knowledge of Christ Jesus is the foundation and source of enduring and deep and beautiful morality.   What can compare with the knowledge of Christ herein ? " All things " are less than nothing in comparison with it.   Never rest till you know Christ as Paul defines knowledge of Him.   To know Christ is to have the supreme possession. How excellent is this excellency!

IV. The excellency, the superiority, the surpassingness of the knowledge of Christ Jesus appears in this also. IT IS SO INFLUENTIAL A KNOWLEDGE.

After all, this is the final test of knowledge—what does it work? Is it influential? And what are its influences? There is knowledge that is no power worth the name. How does the knowledge of Christ Jesus work? This might happily be illustrated in many delightful instances. In the immediate context a number of the effects of this knowledge appear. I will but single out for our present purpose the two typical workings which are named in the verse of which my text is part.

(a) The knowledge of Christ creates *obedience*. Paul calls the Christ he knows so well "my Lord." No man ever yet had "a believing acquaintance with Christ" except "as Lord." To trust Christ and to live Christ is to obey Christ. "My Lord" is a loved title by which the Christian believer designates Christ. They who know Christ ever obey Him. He becomes the Ruler of their life. And the more they know Him, they the more absolutely obey Him. What a superiority attaches to the knowledge of Christ Jesus! It creates obedience. Knowing Christ I enshrine Him as my Lord. He regulates my life. He has me wholly at His command. He finds me ever in willing bonds at His blessed feet. Do you so know Christ as to call Him Lord? He is not known of you except you can say "my Lord." The knowledge of Christ involves the obedience of Christ. Test your knowledge by your obedience.

(β) The knowledge of Christ evokes *endurance*. See how graphically this is exemplified in Paul's own case. It might be easy to affirm that all things pale before the knowledge of Christ. But Paul had given abundant proof of his faith. He had lived out his strong conviction. He had proved his creed by deed; his tremendous creed by sacrificial deed. "For whom I have suffered the loss of all things." The figure is a very striking one. It is an illustration from the Law Courts. It might be expressed, "I was sentenced to the loss of all things." Paul was arraigned before the judge. He was charged with the high crime of being a follower of Christ. He pleaded guilty to the charge. He was fined right heavily. Exorbitant damages were extorted. "All things" were taken from him. Everything that he had

reckoned dear and desirable. " I have suffered
the loss of all things." With Paul it is no case
of boastings. He is not avowing what he might
under given circumstances do. He has done it!
He has endured to the ultimate point. So has
he known Christ, that for Him he has paid down
as damages "all things." What an excellency
has the knowledge of Christ which can command
such endurance! When men know Him they can
part with their all. Nothing has wrought such
fortitude, such brave self-abnegation, as the knowledge of the Saviour.

I commend its supreme superiority because of
its incomparable influence. It is the most influential force of time. Judge it by the obedience
and endurance it inspires. What else is to be
named with it in this regard? It must be a
splendid quality which creates such devotion.
What profit is it, men ask, that we know Christ
Jesus? The reply is manifold and exhaustive.
But what need have we of ampler witness than
this—to know Christ is to have life moulded
by Him who is the wisdom and the power of
God: to know Christ is to be inspired with
an endurance which shall not quail even at the
loss of all things.

Be ours to show that we know Christ by

making Him absolute Lord of our lives, and by enduring all we may be called to endure for His dear
sake. Deeds tell forth His praise as no words
can do. The argument of a loyal and sacrificial
life is unanswerable. The sweetest psalm we have
it in our power to raise is a godly, righteous,
and self-forgetting life.

V. My final word shall be exhortative : THE
KNOWLEDGE OF CHRIST JESUS IS UNIVERSALLY
ATTAINABLE.

Of which of the best things of life can this
be affirmed ? Is wealth possible to all ? Is culture ?
Is love ? Is fame ? These the world reckons its
best things. But they are for the few, or if for
many not for most. But all may know Christ
Jesus, and thus secure the highest, the eternal
good. Truly we may accord with Paul's eulogy
of the excellency—the superiority—the surpassingness of this knowledge. All may see God in
Christ. All may have a complete and everlasting
salvation. All may realize and illustrate the potent
influences of this knowledge. "Whosoever" is
the limitless appeal of the gospel. A personal
believing appropriation of Christ is possible to
every man. The Spirit of God waits to work
this blessed work in every breast. Oh, let us glory

more and more in the free grace of God. The gospel appeal is an illumined circle whose comprehensive sweep takes in the fulness of mankind. May every preacher preach this unrestricted and glorious gospel! May every soul believe it! When Christ shall cleave the skies in Second Advent glory, may He find multitudes gladly awaiting Him because justified by His knowledge!

Have all my readers realised "the excellency of the knowledge of Christ Jesus"? Or has Christ to say to us as He said to one, long time ago, "Have I been so long time with you, and yet hast thou not known Me?" He has indeed been a long time with us. Our parents brought Him to us in our privileged childhood. So did our teachers. So did the ministers whose ministrations arrested us in those early and eager years. Yes. He has been a long time with us. But do we know Him? Long with us, but unknown to us. Great God what an irony is is this! Whilst haply He is still with us, we will surely acquaint ourselves with Him. We will joy and rejoice in the excellency of His knowledge. All else is common clay beside this wedge of Ophir.

IV

"THE LAST AND GREATEST OF THE BEATITUDES"

"Blessed are they that have not seen, and yet have believed."
JOHN XX. 29.

WHAT is blessedness? It is spiritual happiness. It is that deep calm of gladness which is spiritual in its origin and in its maintenance.

This is the heritage of those who, not having seen, yet have believed. And it is the higher blessedness. It is contrastive. Thomas had insisted on sight as an aid to faith. The concession was granted to him. He saw the Risen One, and believing, cried in a passion of adoration, "My Lord and my God!" And he was blessed, Everyone who believes is blessed. But his was not the supreme blessedness. "Jesus saith unto him, Thomas, because thou hast seen Me, thou hast believed : blessed are they that have not seen, and yet have believed." That is the crowning blessed-

ness. They have the noblest beatitude who have
not seen, and yet have believed. Bishop Westcott
called my text "the last and greatest of the beatitudes." A wonderful beatitude it is! It looks
backward, and includes all the Old Testament
believers ; it looks forward, and we who in these
days believe are included too. Every one of us
may come within the radiant circle of this sublime beatitude.

I. CONSIDER THE CHARACTERISTIC WHICH
EVOKES BEATITUDE.

Not seeing, yet believing. Thomas had reached
faith by a sensuous path. He had received earthly
aids. He had seen. The vision of the flesh had
prepared the way for the vision of the spirit. And
so far so good. But there is a peculiar beatitude
upon such as achieve faith and sustain faith by
purely spiritual methods. Faith attained through
sense is blessed, but faith attained apart from sense
has yet higher blessedness. When my believing
owes nothing to fleshly seeing I am graced and
glorified with "the last and greatest of the beatitudes." The faith which wins God's brightest smile
is the faith which is first, midst, and last spiritual.
" Blessed are they that have not seen, and yet have
believed." Faith which does not depend on sense

is a characteristic dear to God. The immediate reference is to belief in the risen Christ, but the principle applies to all the spiritual entities. It is a principle operant in every zone of the spiritual world. To believe any spiritual reality without having seen is to evoke this choice beatitude.

It is a blessed estate which is theirs who have believed without having seen *physically*. This is the portion of all present-day believers. We have none of us seen Christ as to the flesh. At times we judge ourselves disadvantaged thereby. But no! Christ says we are supremely advantaged. We are blessed with a distinctive blessedness. We have really lost nothing by not being alive when Christ was incarnate here. Oh, how we should like to have seen Him! If we could have basked in His smile, or heard His voice, or even felt the rustle of His seamless robe as He flitted past us on the highway. Had we seen we would indeed have believed! Ah! so we reason. But it is a meaner faith which is so inspired. " Blessed are they that have not seen, and yet have believed."

What is true of believing Christ is true concerning all the spiritual objects of faith. God. The heavenly home. Any spiritual truth. The quality which draws down beatitude is a faith which is independent of materialistic props. Flesh can only see flesh. The eyes of the body only see the meaner things of the universe. Oh to be in no wise the slaves of the visible, but the free men of the unseen! Not to see and yet to believe is for the spirit to triumph over the flesh.

But I think the contrast is not intended to be merely between physical sight and faith, but also between all kinds of sight and faith. "Blessed are they that have not seen"—in any sense—" and yet have believed."

They evoke the beatitude who have not seen *imaginatively,* and yet have believed. A vivid imagination may be a way to faith, and by that romantic road some have reached faith. But it is blessed to believe without any imaginative vision either as a cause or support of faith.

Imagination is a great means of grace. We lose much in our religious life for lack of it. That wonderful faculty which images things is one of God's best gifts. It must be freely allowed that there is an element of imagination in faith. But some confound the two and treat them as synonymous. In no wise are they such. Imagination is an ingredient of faith, but only an ingredient. I believe Christians often make themselves sad whom God hath not made sad because they confuse imagination and faith. We think we have lost our faith because we find our imagination dull or blind. But there may be a real believing where there is no imaginative seeing, and to believe though we cannot *so* see is to inherit the last and greatest of the beatitudes.

There are believers whose faith owes nothing to imagination. They did not believe because they first saw with the eyes of their imagination. They are blessed.

So there are believers who keep on believing despite the fact that they do not see imaginatively. They too are blessed. Faith reigns though imagination is dead.

Cheer thee, believing friend, who canst not see imaginatively ! You trust what you cannot image. You believe that which your imaginative vision cannot pourtray. You have the Lord's beatitude. Do not say you have decreased in faith because imagination's eye is filmed. Do not reckon your faith greater because your imagination is clearer. Believe without regard to imagining. "Blessed are they that have not seen (imaginatively), and yet have believed."

May I not read this text yet another way ? "Blessed are they that have not seen *intellectually*, and yet have believed." Some have exercised faith as the result of intellectual perception.

They saw with "the eyes of the understanding," and then they believed. But others owe no debt to their brain for their faith. They never saw intellectually, but they have believed. They are blessed. Certain believers are ever supporting their faith by means of intellectual vision. And faith is blessed howsoever it be created and sustained. But many believers are called to go all their days believing without intellectually seeing. They are blessed. A faith shut up to the spiritual is a faith crowned with royal beatitude.

This is the cross, which some Christians must carry all their life long. They seldom, if ever, see intellectually. Their belief has no intellectual reassurance, or next to none. But they bravely believe on, and they are blessed. Do you see little intellectually of the things which are most surely believed among us? Do you yet believe? Blessed you are. The Lord saith it. I may believe where intellectual vision fails. I may believe when I cannot understand. I am not saved by comprehension or even by apprehension. I am saved by faith. Trust the great things you cannot discern with the understanding, and keep on trusting, though you never clearly discern. Then "the last and greatest of the beatitudes" will flood your life with morning. Let us advance a step further and read this text thus: "Blessed are they that have not seen *orthodoxly*, and yet have believed. Let no man discredit orthodox vision of religious truth. It must count for much to see as the majority of the saints see. To behold what the Catholic Church beholds must be a sacred privilege. But some honest and earnest believers cannot thus see. Strive as they may they fail to perceive as the greater number do. They do not glory in their "heterodoxy," they mourn it. They "have not seen," and sorrowfully acknowledge their inability to see. But they have believed. The redeeming Christ in all His risen glory is the only ground of all their hope. They cannot see the eternal things as most of their brethren see, but they have like precious faith with them. Theirs is the grand beatitude. They are blessed of Christ for evermore.

I said this attitude of believing without seeing may be assumed in relation to various spiritual realities. Look at certain cases in point. In the matter of *personal salvation* it is true that some believe without having seen. Assurance is the high privilege of every Christian. All may have the witness of the Spirit, a direct supernatural testimony to their acceptance with God. But some of the choicest Christians live and die without

such inward evidence. They do not see. They
" have not seen." Yet they believe. All their
trust is in the Lord that bought them. Assuredly
they are blessed.

This is true of *entire sanctification*. Every
believer may have that deeper, higher life which
Wesley loved to describe as " perfect love." To
the personal realization of this high grace each
Christian should believingly strain every nerve.
Often an earnest soul says, " I cannot see how
I can be Christianly perfect here. Were I cleansed
from all my sordidness, and sensuousness, and pride,
and all noxious forms of selfhood, I should not
know myself. I cannot see it." My friend, do
you believe the mighty Saviour can do it for you,
and is willing to do it for you? " Yes, I believe."
Then you are blessed. You shall yet receive
" the sanctification without which no man shall
see the Lord." You have not seen, and yet have
believed.

How frequently this characteristic is manifested
in relation to *the supply of temporal need*. You
have a peculiar business exigency at present.
A great and affrighting difficulty stares you
in the face. " Can God furnish a table in the
wilderness ? " you cry. " Can He make Rephidim
sparkle with pellucid springs? Can He cut a

door in the remorseless rocks that ring me round ? "
You do not see it. But do you believe it ? "Yes
I believe it." Then blessed are you, for, not having
seen, you yet have believed.

Is this not peculiarly so in respect of that
sweet mystery of ageless life, and serene rest, and
delectable joy, and unwearying service which we
call *heaven* ? Oh, if we could see that better land !
Could we but catch the shimmer of the shining
shore beyond the stormy sea ! But we have *not
seen*. Neither physically, nor imaginatively, nor
intellectually, nor perchance even orthodoxly, have
we seen. Yet we believe. We know that the
keeping of Sabbath remaineth. That deathless
life beyond death is our dearest faith. It is a
mercy we cannot see it literally else should we
lose all zest for life and service here. Earth
would be finally spoiled for us. We have the
higher blessedness. We believe without having
seen.

"Blessed are they that have not seen, and yet
have believed." This is an historical fact, for the
most blessed men and women of past days were
such as believed without seeing. We have known
many such and been appreciant of their blessedness. It is an experimental fact. *Our* most
blessed moments have been our believing moments.

We saw least and believed most, we reached the
highest crests of blessedness.

Know ye this more and ever more surely, that
for us all and for us evermore this is the one
path to blessedness.   Be a great believer, and you
shall have a joy that no man taketh from you.

Such is the characteristic which evokes " the
last and greatest of the beatitudes."

II. Ponder the Nature of the Beatitude.

Attempt to analyze the flower—the heaven.
What are some of the elements which make up
this blessedness ?   Very superficial must our
analysis be.   The blessedness of the man who
believes without seeing is surely that of *inward
illumination*.   What the sight of the bodily eyes
and of the understanding and of the imagination
fails to discern, God reveals to the believer's heart.
The Society of Friends speak of " the inward light."
It is a fine phrase, and indicates a finer experience.
If I submit not to see, and am content to believe,
I shall have a divine light on the great things
of the universe.   " God is the Lord who hath
showed us light."   The Christian believer has a
wonderful knowledge which no unbeliever possesses.
God illumines his heart on the purpose of life.
On the secret of eternal weal.   On the meaning

of death. On the rapture of the beyond. I often think we Christians lose great comfort and strength for lack of realising the illumination of God which we have received. "We have an unction of the Holy One, and we all know." The believer sees more on his knees than the non-believer of acutest intellect can discern if he stand on tiptoe. Cometh this blessedness on you? Dr. Maclaren is assuredly right when he affirms, "They say seeing is believing, but in truth believing is seeing." Believe in the Lord Jesus Christ, and you are blessed, for you have an illuminated soul.

A manifold enjoyment of Christ is a large component of this blessedness. The believer draws such pure delight from the Lord in whom he trusts. How grandly Peter states it! "Whom having not seen *ye love.*" The loving of Christ is such unalloyed pleasure. None can know the rapture save only they who experience it. "In whom, though now ye see Him not, yet believing, *ye rejoice.*" And how splendid the quality of the joy: "with joy unspeakable and full of glory." Joy in Christ! Joy that cannot be spoken! Joy shot through with glory! Is not this blessedness? The so-inclusive enjoyment of Christ is a rich element in the believer's blessedness.

The sense of transfigured character goes far to

constitute this blessedness. He who believes
thereby gains the secret of holiness. Faith is
evermore the root of noble character. The man
who believes becomes. His nature, already regenerated, is eternally being "changed from glory
to glory." Oh, is not this a large portion of
Christian blessedness? Belief in manifested God
secures godlikeness.

The believer's blessedness is that of *a restful
conscience*. He has received the Atonement. He
has realized that his Lord was "delivered for"
his "offences" and "raised for" his "justification."
This certitude is a quiet haven for the conscience
so long tossed with tempest. Such a haven is
"commodious to winter in." Nothing calms conscience save believing God in Christ. Believe,
and your conscience no longer condemns. "There
is now no condemnation to them that are in
Christ Jesus." This is of a truth a solid contribution to blessedness.

True comfort amid life's disabilities is another
and precious part of a believer's blessedness.
When we believe we unseal the deepest fount of
consolation. Faith is the supreme solace. Our
crosses may be heavy, our life may be "dipt
in baths of hissing tears," but to believe the gospel
is to know strong comfort. Verily this again

is blessedness. What is more precious than comfort when shocks, and losses, and sore tribulation assail? Nor do we ever touch the spring of genuine and potent solace till we believe. Believe, and you have a refreshing fountain in the heart, better far than any fountain by the way.

The believer has a grasp of *abiding good*, and this yet further builds up the goodly fane of his blessedness. One of life's greatest problems is to find a permanent good. All tenure on earth is insecure. Evanescence is stamped on all things here. "Fading is the sinner's pleasure." But the believer has gripped everlastingness. His city is on a rock which never disintegrates, however overwhelming the tempest. He can afford to let the earth and the heavens pass away. His foothold is on the immutable. He could "smile to see a burning world." His wealth can never take to itself wings and fly away. He has in himself an enduring substance. The believer's blessedness is the blessedness of the permanent.

Have all my readers this blessedness? Can you by happy experience fill in the opulent details of the scene I have so roughly etched? Seek ye to be blessed. Rest not till the Master saith "Blessed" of you. Only a blessedness such as appertains to faith is blessedness indeed. See to it that you have a resplendent heaven of beatitude in your heart.

III. Contemplate the Reason of the Beatitude.

Why are they blessed who have not seen, and yet have believed? Explain if but in hurried sentences the secret of this "last and greatest of the beatitudes."

I assign this as a reason: *Such have accepted God's spiritual method.* God has ever been seeking to educate us into the spiritual. This is the meaning of all disciplinary history. God will have man to live by the spiritual. And how does man live by the spiritual save by believing? "See," cries the world. "Believe" is God's command. They who believe not having seen adopt God's programme. They are scholars in His school, and follow His system of education. Such *must* be blessed. It were inconceivable that a man who falls in with the divine method should be unblest. Have you complied with God's injunction? Do you live joyfully acquiescent in God's spiritual system?

No marvel the believers are blessed: *they please God.* Nothing so delights God as does

faith. It is the choicest gift we can offer Him.
It is to Him more golden than purest gold.
None can please God without faith, so the
Scripture plainly affirms. None can fail to please
God who believe. You cannot conceive that a
man who pleases God can miss blessedness. It
must follow, else were the foundations of things
destroyed. Please God, and the golden gates
of beatitude will open to you of their own
accord.

*The power of the risen Lord works in the
believer.* This is a further reason of the blessedness such enjoy. If I believe Christ I receive
Christ. This is the great mystical fact of
Christianity. He then energizes in my guilty
and helpless soul. Then am I blessed beyond
all blessing. This is the great fontal secret of
beatitude. Seeing can never enrich as believing
can, for believing invests the soul with the all-
power of the glorified Saviour. Blessedness so
created can never wither. It blooms for aye.

We may look in another direction for a reason
of the believer's blessedness.

*Upon such the highest experiences of life have
not been lost.* Spiritual experiences are life's
loftiest experiences. Alas! though they come in
rich profusion, they are lost upon multitudes.

God seems to waste His breath in breathing upon men. But happily redundant grace is justified of God's believing children. God has spoken and they have heard. The Spirit has striven and they have surrendered. They have felt the divineness of the Scriptures, and have gladly bowed beneath their spell. They have seen the cross, and henceforth they can see nothing else. Blessed they must be. It is sweetly inevitable. God must bless unto the ages of the ages souls that have responded to the highest.

A final reason why believers are blessed lies in the sublime fact that *they are independent of the outward*. They have discovered that the outward does not hold the central good. They are assured that the unseen is the real and the eternal. Most lives are victimized by the ephemeral outward. They are rooted in the visible. But the man who believes the unseen has a leash on the abiding. Did the outward lessen, the believer's blessedness would not diminish. Did the outward perish, such would retain their felicity and increase it. Oh, understand the simple yet profound fact that true blessedness cometh from independence of the outward. Do not live in the transient. Seek and cultivate " life which is life indeed." Pray without ceasing to be free of the outward. Sight and things seen shall vanish. "He that doeth the will of God abideth for ever." Said rare Samuel Rutherford, "Build your nest on no tree here, for God has sold the whole forest over to death." Learn that grim yet sanative lesson and you shall know a secret of boundless blessedness.

Have you taken the precaution to adopt that measure which creates blessedness? Pray God to help you to believe, and yours shall be a reasonable and immortal beatitude.

"Blessed are they that have not seen, and yet have believed." All their earthly days they are blessed. They have an inner day which cannot die. Their beatitude persists through all the changing scenes of life. Have we not seen its mild glory gleam amid darkest shades?

But how blessed shall believers be at length! This "last and greatest of the beatitudes" has its full fruition in heaven. God bids us walk by faith, and not by sight, in this time-sphere, and He assures us that in another and far more glorious world we shall have splendid sight. Faith shall be lost in sight of a quality here unknown and unimagined. God asks us to renounce sight here and we shall receive it there. Be content to lack sight awhile and you shall possess it to all eternity. Believe to the end though you see

not, then in God's time you shall see God's face—
to see it will be to see all things we could desire
to see. Struggle on, brave believer, and shortly
thou shalt see!

Wandering in a village churchyard, I saw a
lovely white marble cross which marked the grave
of a little child, and engraved on the shining stone
was the repeated exclamation, " I see, I see."
Evidently this had been the last word of the sweet
immortal as it lost itself in light. " I see, I see."
We have heard the passing believer cry, " I see,
I see." Wait but a little while, my believing
brother, and you too shall rapturously exclaim,
" I see, I see."

When we outsoar the shadow of this night we
shall all songfully say, " I see, I see."

V

A GREAT EVANGELICAL DETERMINATION

" For I determined not to know anything among you, save Jesus Christ, and Him crucified."—1 COR. ii. 2.

THIS is autobiographic. Probably Paul wrote in the spring of the year 58. And he records a great evangelical determination which he had registered before high heaven. The determinations of the Bible deserve careful study. None, however, is more solemn and august and inspiring than this. Can *we* rise to the height of this great argument ?

Very startling is this avowal. In view of his ministry at Corinth, Paul had determined doubtless very much, but this supremely, " not to know anything, save Jesus Christ, and Him crucified." He will not know even Jesus Christ save in one aspect. That is the idea. One of our best exegetes thus renders the words : " And even Him *as having been crucified.*" It is the crucified Christ alone he will know. Observe the far-reaching word

71

"know." Not merely does he refuse to speak on any other theme, but he will "know" none other. The crucified Saviour shall fill the whole horizon of his mind and heart. He will, so to say, severely limit his Christology to this phase: "Even Him as having been crucified." It was without controversy a portentous determination. Truly the crucified Christ must be the transcendent spiritual truth and power when Paul so resolved concerning Him.

Was this an exceptional determination? Some have singled out the words "among you" as signifying something out of the usual run of Paul's ministry. They have represented him as saying, "I determined to do among you for special reasons what I am not accustomed to do in my general ministry." But I cannot accept such an interpretation. Everywhere Paul did as he proposed to do in Corinth. A severe and grand constancy marked his incomparable ministry. I regard this "among you" as not exceptional but emphatic. He resolves to do with specialty of earnestness in Corinth what he everywhere does. The trumpet shall sound out the dominant note more sonorously here than anywhere. The central theme shall be more luminously central than before. Not improbably this determination of St. Paul's represents a temptation conquered, a soul-conflict won. To such an one as he it would be a trial of spirit to contemplate service in such a city as Corinth. Corinth was a centre of fashion. Shall he essay to appeal to the fashionable crowd with Christ *crucified* as the central theme? Will he not repel them thus? May he not emphasize other aspects of Christ which will be attractive and not repellant? Thus the evil one would ply him. But the God of peace crushed Satan under his feet, and his splendid " I determined " rings out. Corinth was an æsthetic city. Its architecture is a proverb still, and its brasses are famous now. Corinth was an intellectual city. Its typical Greek love of philosophy all men know. An opulent commercial city too. Shall he not soften the truth and smooth his message? Will not taste, and culture, and materialism, and wealth resent the preaching of " Him crucified "? Mayhap. But " I determined," cries this hero of the cross. He will cry out and shout in the delicate ears of Corinth nothing but the crucified Lord.

And was there not scope for such a concentred message? With all its art and culture and affluence Corinth was abominably corrupt. To " Corinthian-ize " was a synonym for lust. Corinth seethed with guilt, and was sodden with sin. Its cheek was painted gaily, but its heart was diseased. Corinth was a "hyperbole of sin," and Paul was a good physician. He could diagnose accurately and prescribe unerringly. He knew that to dilate on Christ's character and teachings and lovely deeds, would not effect the salvation of the gay town. Only Christ "as having been crucified" could accomplish such a miracle. Penitence would only be evoked and simple faith by such a message. Hence from such a message alone could pardon and regeneration and sanctification spring. Therefore, says the great evangelist, "I determined not to know anything among you, save Jesus Christ, and Him crucified."

Was this a narrow determination? Such it has been pronounced, but with arrant injustice, It is to be feared that an ignorant and narrow evangelism has often misapplied these capacious words. Let us strive, as the Holy Spirit shall illumine us, to show that there is no narrowness in this splendid decision. It is spacious with firmamental infinity. The very catholicity of God breathes in this heroic evangelical determination.

I. PAUL DETERMINED NOT TO KNOW ANYTHING SAVE THE CRUCIFIED AS HIS DOMINATING IDEA.

It is not that he refuses to think or realize or

teach anything else, but that he refuses to allow anything else the ruling place. It is a question not of exclusion but of domination. He will know no truth about Christ, nor any truth, as the supreme truth. The Crucified shall reign in his intellect, and heart, and will, and speech. Supremacy in his ministry shall be the unquestioned right of the crucified Saviour. There shall be no question as to the dominating verity.

It may be said to be a matter of supremacy and relativity. Or it may be described as a question of comparison; in comparison with the Crucified Paul will know no other theme.

I am persuaded this is the true exposition of this brave determination. Perhaps here, as often, illustration is the best exposition. To-morrow I have to preach at such and such a city. I have many other things to do to-morrow. I have to answer letters from saints who are too unworldly to enclose a stamp for reply. I have a sick one to visit. I have promised to take my children for an outing. But I determined that I will know nothing to-morrow—dominatingly—save preaching the word of God in yonder city. All else relatively to that is nothing. That is my ruling idea. Thus Paul resolved not to know anything among the Corinthians save the crucified Christ. His crowning teaching was for ever settled as being the atoning Saviour.

Were this not the meaning of his determination then he were inconsistent with striking inconsistency. For he " knew " many things among the Corinthians. I have noted sixteen different subjects on which he spoke to the Corinthians, as is shown in his epistles, and there are more. Yet Paul says he determined not to know anything save Christ crucified! It was the dominating consideration. All else was subordinate to this, and depended upon this for its sanction and inspiration. My friends, that is practical, intelligent, and broad evangelism! That is the type of evangelism our age needs. On many topics the preacher must expatiate, but his dominating doctrine must be Christ crucified. Change the centre and our word will be of none effect. Even Christ will profit us nothing except we lay the supreme emphasis upon Him "as having been crucified." Only the *redeeming* Christ is the true centre of Christian preaching. Thus it was with Paul, and so it must evermore be with us. But is it so? Would it strike the most casual observer that the *dominant* note of modern preaching is Christ crucified? Not Christ crucified as a martyr, but as a sin-bearer? Oh, let us unite with Paul in this evangelical determination! Be all else sub-ordinate to this. Let all else be tested by this touchstone. Measure everything by this infallible standard. Nothing can arrest the world's guilt and destroy its sin but "Christ as having been crucified." Paul's gospel is ours: be Paul's determination ours.

II. PAUL DETERMINED NOT TO KNOW ANY-THING SAVE THE CRUCIFIED AS THE GROUND OF SALVATION.

He will have the Corinthians to be saved—evangelically and ethically. To have their sins blotted out and righteousness attained is his absorbing ministerial purpose in the careless, pleasure-loving, mammon-worshipping city. He would have Corinth a city of God.

If this blest consummation is ever to be it can only be by the dynamic of Christ crucified. Faith in the atoning Lord alone can effect so glorious a transformation. We may know "Jesus" among men, but that cannot save men. We may know "Christ," but that cannot save men. We may know "Jesus Christ," but even that has no redeeming power. It is "Him as having been crucified" which saves the world. Hence Paul's great determination.

Would Paul not refer to other influences as helpful in respect of salvation? Assuredly he would, and we know he did. There are "things that accompany salvation." There are also things that precede salvation. Many injunctions did Paul lay upon the Corinthians if they would be saved. Much they must do and much they must refuse to do. But all this was subsidiary. The dominating truth for salvation is Christ crucified. Repentance, restitution, watchfulness, many a rule of sacred discipline—these must be observed if men would be saved; but the supreme thing is to look in simple faith to the crucified Saviour.

Men and brethren, let us to-day and always keep within the lines of Paul's determination. Much else is necessary to salvation, but "Christ crucified" is dominatingly necessary. It is not enough to preach and believe Christ, it must be "Christ as having been crucified." No evangelism can permanently succeed if it be not evangelical. The head and front of it must be the Crucified. Lest men perish for lack of knowledge, publish the death divine everywhere and always as God's good news of salvation!

Let Christians, too, remember that all through their course they are saved by nothing else but the merit of the crucified Christ. Salvation at every stage is by this and this only. We are in danger of forgetting this so essential truth. There is a fatal tendency to suppose that at the beginning we are saved by faith in the Crucified, but that as the years pass we are saved by our own good works. Assuredly this is not so. At every step of the heavenward road we are saved by Christ " as having been crucified." The ripest saint is not accepted for his ripeness, but for the Redeemer's sake. From start to close of our pilgrimage we are accepted "in the Beloved." Blessed are they who know nothing as the ground of salvation from the city of destruction to the King's Palace but " Jesus Christ and Him crucified."

When the end of life comes we must know nothing dominatingly but this. Memories of " something attempted, something done " for Christ's dear sake will soothe and cheer us, but our only basis of hope for eternal blessedness must be the crucified Saviour. " Die on justification, not on sanctification," was the wise evangelical counsel of one of the greatest of divines. On justification Wesley died. On justification Spurgeon died. Thus die we all. In view of our final exodus, let ·us say with mellow emphasis, " I determined

not to know anything among you, save Jesus
Christ, and Him *crucified.*

III. PAUL DETERMINED NOT TO KNOW ANY-
THING SAVE THE CRUCIFIED AS THE SUBJECT
OF RELIGIOUS TEACHING.

It is to religious teaching Paul specially alludes
He is thinking of his "speech" and his "testimony." Seldom was his life-passion absent from
his thoughts. Paul was the patriarch of preachers.
In anticipating his ministry at Corinth he determined not to know anything dominatingly as
his subject save the crucified Lord. As a matter
of fact he did know much else in his Corinthian
teaching, but he knew nothing as the supreme
and crowning subject. This was his central instrumentality, his principal weapon. He held that
the solution of all problems was in this wondrous
truth. He brought everything to this test: strife
in the Church; Christian work; the loathsomeness
of sensuality; the reverence of the body; the
significance of example; Christian liberty with
its permissions and limitations; philanthropy;—
these and all other questions he settled at the
cross. He proclaimed that the programme of
the human race was drawn up at Calvary. Every-

thing, according to Paul, was to be determined by the hallowed cross.

And was he not right ? Is not Paul the minister's pattern to the end of the age ? Does not every gospel herald wisely to determine not to know anything as the royal theme save the crucified Christ ? Mrs. Humphrey Ward has remarked that " to reconceive Christ is the special task of our age." She is a blind guide in so saying. To recover the Pauline conception of Christ is the special task of our age, and the sooner we do it the better for our age. When the Crucified as a subject of religious teaching acquires domination again the Church and the world will be created anew.

All spiritual and moral and social problems gather their true light from our Lord's cross. Study all things in that shaded light ; speak all your messages from that sacred vantage-ground. If any have forsaken the redeeming cross, to it let them heartily return. All teaching is fore-doomed to failure which is not inspired by and referred to the crucified Christ. " Back to Christ," they cry. Yes ! but back to Christ " as having been crucified." The disappointing moral tone in Christian circles ; the chill atmosphere in many churches ; the lethargy in sacred endeavour ; the dearth of conversions—unquestioned except by blindest optimists ;—these ills are only curable at the cross. O henchmen of the Christ, swear new devotion to the wondrous cross! Know nothing else as your regnant thought and teaching! Glory ye only in the cross!

IV. PAUL DETERMINED NOT TO KNOW ANYTHING SAVE THE CRUCIFIED AS THE CENTRE OF PERSONAL RELIGIOUS LIFE.

You cannot fathom this "know" of his; he would "know" nothing else. None can exhaust the meaning of that term. It covers every part of his being and every aspect of his ministry. Whilst he tarried in the wealthy and voluptuous city of Corinth, neither in his outward nor inward life would he allow any centre of religion but the crucified Christ. Again let me say the reference is to what is dominant. Nothing should *rule* his religious life but this ; never would he allow its supremacy to be discounted or even challenged.

Paul would know nothing else *as the ruling subject of meditation.* On other themes he pondered, but most on this. This atmosphered for him every other matter of thought. He was great in the holy art of contemplation ; and this greatness, like all his greatness, was originated and enhanced at the cross. How doest thou in this regard, my friend? What musings hast thou at Calvary? Is the crucified thy predominant meditation? When our thoughts within us are clustered around the cross as sorrowful yet hopeful spectators, we are blessed beyond compare. Be ashamed, O vagrant mind of mine, that thou art so little at the cross! Determine, then, to meditatively know nothing else but thy crucified Lord.

Paul scorned to know anything else *as the basis of prayer.* When he prayed—and when did he not pray?—it was in the name of Christ, " and even Him as having been crucified." Paul's prayers as recorded are beyond price. But what of his private and unrecorded prayers? Who can imagine their richness and copiousness and pre-valency? And the open secret is that he would know nothing else as the ground of them all. Paul prayed because Christ died for him. The crucified was the inspiration of his prayers. He pleaded as his insuperable plea his dying Lord. He asked to be heard of God because for him Christ died. The Crucified was the argument of his prayers. The Crucified gave wideness and urgency and tenderness to those matchless prayers of Paul. Do you understand experimentally what this meaneth? We restrain prayer because we know other than Christ crucified in our devotional life. Our prayers are deficient in victorious quality for the same reason. O man of God, plead the crucified Saviour when thou prayest. May He atmosphere the "inner chamber."

Paul knew nothing but the Crucified *in his study of the Scriptures.* The "book" was "sprinkled with blood" to him. The Bible was indeed as he read it a Crimson Book. To him his redeeming Lord swayed an unchallenged sceptre through the domain of Scripture. He found much else there, but only this supremely. Relatively he knew nothing else in his ceaseless searchings of the written word, "How readest thou? Is thy Bible red with redemption as Paul's was? Eliminate the crucified Lord from either Testament and they are howling wildernesses. Let Him reign there and they are twin Paradises.

Happy souls that have no centre of their religious life but Christ crucified! A church of *such* believers will be a church that shall storm the gates of hell.

V. PAUL DETERMINED NOT TO KNOW ANYTHING SAVE CHRIST CRUCIFIED AS THE MOTIVE AND END OF CHRISTIAN WORK.

The "for" with which he introduces his

evangelical resolve indicates this distinctly. It looks back to the opening verse of the chapter. He entered upon his Corinthian ministry in the spirit of his pre-determination. " Excellency of speech or of wisdom " he did not manifest *as motives or ends.* He only knew one motive and one end—" Christ crucified." Of him this was ever true, and never truer than whilst he served in the gospel at Corinth.

Brothers, this is the only adequate and enduring motive. All other motives lack staying power. I shall weary of my ministry and of my life-work except I discharge it, because the Son of God loved me and gave Himself for me. And no other end is worthy. Shall I minister that I may shine? Such shining would be hell-gleams. No work of mine, however supposedly sacred, can effect real good except it be wrought for the glory of Him who died for me. As Robertson finely expresses it, " that which is to be a temple of God must never have the marble polluted with the name of the architect or builder."

Search we our hearts as to our motive and end. Know we nothing but Christ and Him crucified. That as motive, and that as end, and that alone will stand the flaming revelation of the tremendous day.

VI. PAUL DETERMINED NOT TO KNOW ANYTHING SAVE CHRIST CRUCIFIED AS THE PATTERN OF CHARACTER.

He resolved to live among the Corinthians in the spirit of the dying Lord. He understood what we all so need to realise, that the cross is a passion as well as a creed, a life as surely as a doctrine, a temper as distinctively as a theology.

Paul modelled his life according to the pattern showed him in Mount Calvary. He lived the loving, sacrificial, ministrant life. He spent self-less days. He commended His cross-possessed mind by his cross-possessed character.

Let this be our final lesson. Be this our immediate and abiding determination. Other patterns of life and character we may know, but this we *must* know. We may not know any other as our dominating ideal. Oh to catch and surrender not this sacred passion!

If we cannot preach Christ and Him crucified we can live Him. I do not ask if our characters suggest Christ to men. I ask if they suggest Him "*as having been crucified.*" If our daily life is redolent of the Atonement we are evangelists of a most sacred order.

Shall we not emulate Paul's great evangelical determination?

Shall we not now and evermore be true knights of the crucified Son of God?

VI

QUENCHED LAMPS

" Also they have . . . put out the lamps."—2 CHRON. xxix. 7.

THAT is very true to-day. The fact which
Hezekiah deplores may well sadden us
also. Historically, as a study of this rich chapter
will show, these words are of ominous interest ;
but prophetically they have accumulated significance. I use the text as a motto. It is not
exposition but appeal I seek. Let us see if it
be not true of our time that "they have . . . put
out the lamps." The text is pertinent now.
All texts are pertinent now.

Ruskin wrote with perennial power of the seven
lamps of Architecture. We contemplate the seven
lamps of religion. They were the lamps of the
temple that Hezekiah's profane fathers quenched.
How many are putting out the seven lamps of
God's great temple now ! What a difference the
lamps make ! Look at Edinburgh by night from

Calton Hill. The lamps illuminate the fair and romantic town. They make it a dream ; a poem amid the gloom. But let the lamps be extinguished in the black bad night, and the beauteous city might be a city of the dead. Do not the lamps count in the home? And what do they stand for in the Church ? Desolate and drear is the temple environed with night, if the lamps be put out. Consider some of the lamps which certain essay to put out, and that too often with fatal success.

I. Evangelical Doctrine is a Lamp which Some have Put Out.

The truth as it is in Jesus is not unfrequently compared in Scripture to a lamp or torch. And what a radiant lamp it is ! The noblest epitaph I know is that of John Owen, the massive philosophic exegete and theologian of the Puritans. In that eloquent eulogium we are told, what we happily know to be the case, that he held up " the effulgent lamp of evangelical truth." A fine phrase, but indicating a far finer reality. A man has lived to splendid purpose who has held up that effulgent lamp. But there be those, and have always been, who have put out the lamp. It is very markedly so now. Paul foretold it clearly. " In the latter

times some shall depart from the faith." He
forewarned the young Timothy, and all young
ministers need such prophecy lest they be swallowed
up of overmuch sorrow. I believe we are living
in "the latter times." Sure I am this sign of
the times is so clear that he may run who readeth.
Many pulpits and many churches have put out
"the effulgent lamp of evangelical truth." No
marvel that godless multitudes have all but glee-
fully extinguished it. Thank God, none can
quench it absolutely, but in relation to themselves
and their circle they have done the sacrilegious
deed. "They have . . . put out the lamps." How
little we hear or read in many quarters concerning
the great "notes" of evangelical doctrine! If the
lamp is not entirely dark, much-prized rays are
missing. If the trumpet is not criminally silent,
full often it gives an uncertain sound. Take
instances. We listen, frequently to our disappointment, for the distinctively Christian conception of
God. The mysterious doctrine of the Holy
Trinity represents the very genius of Christianity.
It is the richest and fullest of theoligies. We
have not a singular God, but a trinal God. Father-
hood. Saving sonship. Ministering spirituality.
These are distinct but not separate personalities in
the one God. Verily an incomparable doctrine of

God. Such a theology should give Christianity a
ceaseless triumph. Dr. Dale expected the next
great revival to come out of that doctrine. It
was a reasonable anticipation, but where are the
signs of its coming?

The deity of Christ cannot be too unequivocally
proclaimed. The distinction between an evangelical and a Unitarian should be always and
everywhere obvious. But is it? Teachers must
be estimated by their omissions as well as by
their affirmations. Did we so estimate we should
often be found exclaiming, "They have . . . put
out the lamps." The ethical Jesus we are made
very familiar with. We are bidden admire the
social Jesus. The teaching Jesus is no unaccustomed figure. But "Jesus, my God," is a vision
concerning which many are sadly reticent. Paul's
Jesus is God. Paul declares it was the blood of
God which redeemed us. Concede less than Paul
conceded and you may conciliate a few sceptics,
but you have put out the lamp.

What of the personality and work of the Holy
Spirit? Are not many Christians unconsciously
Arian in their view of the Spirit? Is the indispen-
sableness of that personal, operative, divine
being realized generally? If William Arthur's
"Tongue of Fire," that immortal classic of experi-

mental theology, were ever in our hand, it would, through grace, save us from putting out the lamp.

Then consider the evangelical doctrine of the death of Christ. Everything in Christianity stands or falls by that. Our Lord's death is the ruddy core of the New Testament. Many preach it and more believe it. But do they preach and believe it evangelically? The cross cannot avail except it be evangelically interpreted. If Christ's death was only a martyrdom it has no saving efficacy. Martyrs are not saviours. The ethics of Calvary are pathetic and lovely in highest degree, but they cannot redeem. I believe the death divine was a sublime substitution. I cannot fathom it—angels cannot—but I accept it with all my intellect, and heart, and will. There is no salvation, either in this world or in any other, except by personal reliance upon the death, the substitutionary death, of the Son of God. We must stand by the evangelical doctrine of the Atonement. Let us, my fellow-preachers, preach it as Spurgeon did, though men sneer at our "theory" as "commercial." Let us expound it as Dr. Denny does, with rare scholarship and felicity of phrase, and devotional insight in his study of "The Death of Christ." Oh, put not out, I beseech you, "the effulgent lamp of evangelical truth."

The ancient priests had to "dress the lamps" in the tent of meeting, and they were to be vigilant that "continually" those sacred lamps were glowing. Such is the pre-eminent function of the ministry, in its narrower and larger definition, to-day. The motto of Caxton, the first great English printer, was, "Let there be light." That must be the motto of evangelical Churchman in these times. God send us more of the evangelical generation of John Owen, who shall hold up to all men "the effulgent lamp of evangelical truth."

Young men and women! go to the churches where this golden lamp shines. Steer clear of those who have put out the lamps. Never mind how "ethical," or "eloquent," or "intellectual," or "up to date" ministers may be, if they "put out the lamps" they are no ministers for you. Many clever gentlemen are engaged in quenching historic and eternal lamps. Avoid them. Let them exercise their darkening art in appropriate solitude. Lamp-*lighters* are the need of these darkling times.

Give God the glory for the widespread irradiation the evangelical lamp doth send forth! In squalid places the light shineth. In splendid places it enhances the splendour. " Let there be light ! " Be this the united and urgent intercession of evangelical believers. And there shall be light. No truce with those who would put out the lamps ! We will denounce them as Hezekiah did. We will undo their ghastly disservice as Hezekiah did. We will be jealous for the lamps.

II. WORSHIP IS A LAMP WHICH SOME HAVE PUT OUT.

If there be a commandment which pervades Scripture more entirely than another, it is this, " Worship God." No lamp of the seven lamps of religion is more needful than this. Without its aureate luminosity we are dark indeed. Public worship is alike an injunction of God and an instinct of man. Of multitudes it may be declared, " They have put out " this " lamp." With what grim eloquence recent census returns of church-attendance speak ! The masses and the classes of Britain are quenching one of the noblest lamps ever kindled by the Father of lights. I do not now seek to assign the reasons of this fatuous proceeding. Probably criticism should begin at the house of God. Is " Welcome " writ

large across every wall of the sanctuary? Do
we preachers preach the most interesting, and
thrilling, and momentous realities as if they
were fictions? Are our sordid lives an anti-climax
to our sublime discourses? These and kindred
inquiries must be honestly answered. But somehow, so help us the Spirit of God, we must
arrest this lamp-quenching propensity. Thank
God, in many places the deleterious tendency
is being restrained. The lamp of worship shines
out here, and yonder, and yonder, with a glory
unknown before. But, oh, people of God, inter-
cede that "men who have understanding of the
times" may be raised up, who shall undo the
work of the moral madcaps who have put out
the lamp.

I am solicitous concerning one element of
worship, the ordinance of preaching. Preaching
is the highest type of worship. They who say,
"We go to church to worship, you go to hear
a sermon," institute an antithesis which is invalid.
Hearing a sermon is profoundest worship. No
other act of worship is so inclusive. It calls
every faculty into exercise. Devout hearing of
a sermon means of necessity prayer, and intro-
spection, and meditation, and communion with
the saints. We do well to be careful of this

mode of worship. Nothing must eliminate illu-
minative, sympathetic, heart-renewing preaching.
May Britain flourish by the preaching of the
word. This is still the "Royal ordinance."
Matthew Henry will have it that by the "putting
out of the lamps" is signified—"the word not
duly read and opened." Watch that lamp! Moses
"lighted the lamps before the Lord." So let
every latter-day Moses do. Brother, quench
not the lamp of worship, else how great the
darkness that shall shroud thy life!

III. The Bible is a Lamp which Some
have Put Out.

"Thy word is a lamp" sang the grateful
Psalmist. No symbol could be more every way
apposite. What an all-illumining lamp it is! A
lamp for the church. A lamp for the home. A
lamp for the office or shop. A lamp for the
lonesome "valley of the shadow," dissipating its
gloom, and flooding it with mellow glory. And
it was the availableness, the homeliness, the utility
for common scenes which God's word evinces
that charmed the Psalmist. He describes it as
"a lamp unto my feet and a light unto my path."
It is not merely a remote illumination, a planetary
flame, an astronomical lustre. It is near, ever

and everywhere helpful; it accommodates itself to my immediate need.

Then how infinite the folly that puts out such a lamp. The character of the Bible is the argument for its preservation. If it be what it is, let it continue to be. No act can be more unpatriotic, unsocial, suicidal, than in any sense to extinguish the lamp which shineth in the dark place of time.

Do we not need, as Churches, to recover the ancient attitude of ardent loyalty and reverence towards the word of God? Bishop Wordsworth (one of the profoundest of scholars) said that many so-called "critics" of the Old Testament treated it as "a culprit at the bar." That is the attitude of some to the Old and New Testament alike. They, forsooth, are the judge, and it is the culprit; they are fain to pronounce a death sentence, but they commute it to penal servitude for life. The attitude of others is that of patronage. They pronounce the Book fairly good on the whole, or "not bad." Thank God for reverent criticism! But away with the criticism, anti-super-naturalistic in its whole spirit, which puts out the lamp. "Higher criticism" may be very good, but is it not time we had a process of contrite criticism? We are the culprit at the bar, and the Bible is the judge. That aforetime attitude is the true attitude. Brethren, pray we without ceasing that we may stand Bible-wards as God would have us stand. Oh, put not out this lamp Divine. Walk ye with humble joy in the light of it.

Have any of us quenched it? Fellow-preachers, have we? Have we preached novels, and Parliamentary legislation, and current events instead of the Holy Book? Oh, let the immortal flame shine forth. Put not out the lamp. Let it flood the temple. Bible-lighted churches are the want of the age. Let it flush the home with its rosy beauty. You commercial men, live your six working days by its guiding light. In its radiance, may all the nations of the earth walk till time shall cease to be.

IV. CHRISTIAN MORALITY IS A LAMP WHICH SOME HAVE PUT OUT.

Christianity is a regeneration that it may be a morality. By the power of the redeeming and indwelling God it creates a splendid ethic. Our religion is a theology, a creed, that it may become a life. Now, Christian character is, and ever has been, the world's finest moral illuminant. "The life was the light of men" is a great avowal, true of the servant as supremely true of the Lord. There is no light like life. It was to life that many of us owed our earliest light—a father's godliness, a mother's gentle piety. The world's greatest evangelising force is Christian character. The only sermon that never wearies us is that of an eloquent life.

There is danger of preaching unevangelical ethics, but there is sorer danger of failing to preach and failing to practise evangelical ethics. The every-day morality of the cross is the true proof of the power of the cross. " He that doeth righteousness is righteous " is the eternal edict of Christianity.

Is there not cause for uneasiness in the im-poverished morality of many Christians? This is no new thing. It is an ancient evil. But what concerns us is that it is also markedly a modern evil. There is a low moral tone, even among evangelical and evangelistic people. If any can successfully deny this, oh, how gladly will we accept his denial! Alas! we fear such denial is impossible. Of how many who name the holy Name is it true that they have quenched the lamp of Christian morality? How sordid and selfish are many professedly Christian lives! How full of envy, malice, and all uncharitableness!

How mean the tricks, and contemptible their
devices, and despicable the wire-pulling of some!
In sacred corporations courses are too frequently
followed which would be scouted by a concourse
of honourable men of the world. O man of God,
flee these things! Put not out the lamp of lovely
living. Let thy words and deeds shine for thy
Saviour. Be it yours to illuminate those about
you. For nothing does the dark world cry more
clamorously than for consistent Christian living.
This argument has no answer. This logic is
irrefragable. Against such there is no law. Every
Christian should be like Job's leviathan, "out of
his mouth" should "go burning lamps." All the
Churches of Christ should be, as Ezekiel's living
creatures, "like the appearance of lamps."

V. Entire Sanctification is another
Lamp which Some have Put Out.

Isaiah, that fervent intercessor and flaming evangelist, was eager for the blissful age when Jerusalem's
"salvation" should be "as a lamp that burneth."
No lamp burns so gloriously and allures so irresistibly as a full salvation. But, alas, of how
many of us is the indictment true, "they have put
out the lamp"! We have spoken of Christian
morality. But we are called to Christian

holiness—a far higher, richer quality of character. We will not quibble as to terminology. Say "Holiness," or "Full Sanctification," or (Wesley's favourite phrase) "Perfect Love," or "Higher Life," or "Second Blessing." Call it what ye will, but possess ye the reality. What a lack of this *complete* Christian life there is! It is rare to meet one who is obviously, though all unconsciously, absolutely surrendered to God; made every way Jesus-like; "filled with the Spirit." Are saints becoming scarcer? Is Pentecostal consecration lapsing? Where are the supernal wind and the mystic flame? Oh that a revival of entire sanctification were in our midst! Would that God might raise up evangelists to the Churches! When we are radiant with inward and outward holiness, then, indeed, shall we be "the light of the world."

VI. Consecrated Home-life is One of the Lamps which Many have Put Out.

What a lovely lamp is this! Ten thousand times ten thousand have been made thereby to be "light in the Lord." Do not observers of the religious signs of the times descry a dimming, if not a quenching, of that lamp? May not the decadence of home religion explain any religious decadence there may be otherwise? "When families pray, Churches prosper." If our family prayers wither, the Church will inevitably fade. Have you an altar in your house? I beg you erect one. By so doing you will effect a solid service for the nation and for the Church. But, above all else, do you live as Christians should at home? Is the law of kindness on your tongue? Are you your best at home? Is your life such that all under the roof shall be likely to be enamoured of your faith and love? Let this lamp be always burning bright.

VII. THE LAMP OF IMMORTALITY SOME HAVE PUT OUT.

Needs there a word to prove this lamp has been and is being put out in this our age? With apparently light heart and willing hand, men quench this lamp. Surely they know not what they do. Tennyson avers that immortality is "the leading light of man," and that this has been so "since our dying race began." It is so of a truth. Then to put out so luminous a lamp must be a criminal act. You surrender New Testament Christianity when you surrender immortality. You do more. You destroy one of the chief inspirations to and supports of morality.

Moreover, you annihilate the strongest solace of weary and wounded lives.

It is here one of Britain's greatest dangers lies. The direst foe of our native land is the man who would put out this lamp. Extinguish this God-lit flame and you create dreariest dulness. The peace, and joy, and dramatic interest of life cease when Sadduceeism is the dogma of the age. Dust will be our food if dust we deem to be our destiny. Quench this lamp, and you will have a generation of pessimists. Our newspapers and magazines dwell much upon the prevalent pessimism. Pleasure is rampant, and yet pessimism is even more rampant. A stange juxtaposition—redundant pleasure and redundant pessimism! Surrender the living hope, put out the lamp of immortality, and no pleasures can shut out the blackness of darkness. But tell a struggling tradesman, a bereaved parent, or husband or wife, a dying man, a youth struggling with base passions : tell such of "life which is life indeed," ageless and victorious life beyond the bounds of death. Tell them of this, and you flash a lamp upon their gloom, the quality of which attests its Divinity. By the grace of God we will not put out this lamp. O sacred fire, burn on amid earth's gloom !

Men and brethren, beware of quenching the

lamps of God. Arise and trim these holy lamps. Should any have put out the lamps, let us re-light them. To extinguish the lamps of a lighthouse on a dark, tempestuous night, were an evil lesser far than to put out the seven lamps of religion, for, whilst the one dastardy would cause bodily wreckage, this would involve the wreck of ransomed souls. Let our lamps be brightly burning. Through the night of doubt and sorrow they shall flash with everlasting glory.

VII

WITNESS TO THE LIVING CHRIST

"It is witnessed that He liveth."—HEB. vii. 8.

"OF whom speaketh the prophet this?" First of Melchisedec, then of Christ Jesus the Lord. This magnificent epistle was a consolation and compensation to the Hebrew Christians. They perchance would deplore the departed glories of Judaism, and mayhap would be cruelly taunted because of the great eclipse. The great idea (most nobly wrought out) of this epistle is to show that the essential glories remain in Jesus the Saviour. The greatness of Christ is the splendid theme of the epistle. In His greater greatness all other greatness fades.

The especial subject of this section of the eloquent and logical epistle is the priesthood of Christ: that priesthood, the holy writer argues, was adumbrated in Melchisedec, that strange, weird, pastoral king-priest of the early days. In no less than seven features was the priesthood of the shadowy Melchisedec superior to that of the Levitical priesthood. My text illustrates the third of those significant particulars: "And here (in the Levitical priesthood) men that die (dying men) receive tithes; but there (in the case of Melchisedec), one of whom it is witnessed that he liveth." The Aaronic priests are transient by reason of death: the greater priest is permanent, for he ever liveth.

Dean Vaughan says, "We see here a sort of blending of type and anti-type." Melchisedec is named, but Christ is intended. And it is to Him that in their final reference these remarkable words apply: "It is witnessed that He liveth." The idea might be yet more emphatically expressed, "It is witnessed, this and no other, that He liveth."

What a witness there is that Jesus liveth! And the witness is on the same lines as that borne to Melchisedec. But it is stronger with immeasurable strength. The witness that Christ liveth throws the witness that Melchisedec liveth into infinite shade. Christ ever does what the typical Melchisedec did, and these deeds witness that He liveth. Christ ever receives what the typical Melchisedec received, and the things offered to Christ bear witness that He liveth. Let us examine and admire the manifold witness. How glorious is the truth that He liveth! What uniqueness has Christ in this? But how little we realize it! Yet it is our great safeguard—our sole basis of assurance. It is because He is the ever-living One that He is able to save them to the uttermost, that come unto God by Him (v. 25). "Unto the consummate end" (Dean Farrar) Christ is able to save because He liveth for ever!

Our inquiry now must be, how is it "witnessed that He liveth"?

I. IT IS WITNESSED BY HOLY SCRIPTURE.

This is the first idea of our text. As it refers to Melchisedec, it asserts that on the pages of God's word it is witnessed that he liveth. It is witnessed in the book of Genesis, in that wonderful fourteenth chapter, wherein the strange tale of Melchisedec is told. It is witnessed in the one hundred and tenth Psalm. It is witnessed abundantly in this notable chapter of this most notable epistle. But the witness in Melchisedec's case is purely negative; indeed, it may be said to be a mystical witness. Melchisedec, as far as the record goes, still lives, for there is no notice of his death. The almost rabbinical conclusion of the writer of the epistle is that, as history is silent concerning the priest-king's death, "it is witnessed that he liveth."

But here, as all through the sacred discussion, there is the blending of type and anti-type of which Dean Vaughan has reminded us, Melchisedec is named, Jesus is thought of. What was negatively true of that ancient figure is positively true of Christ. Mystically applicable to Melchisedec, it is literally applicable to our Lord—"it is witnessed that He liveth."

The Scripture witness to the living Christ is ample, unequivocal, delightsome. You must disprove your Bible before you can discredit the aliveness of Christ. "He liveth" is a pealing proclamation which sounds through the literary shrine of God.

"It is witnessed that He liveth." Yes. We need not leave this strong and glowing chapter to find this witness clear as a sunbeam. Says ver. 3, he "abideth a priest continually," or in "perpetuity." Says ver. 16, "Who is made, not after the law of a carnal commandment, but after the power of an endless life" (literally, "of an indissoluble life"). Says ver. 17, "A priest for ever." Says ver. 21, "A priest for ever." Says ver. 24, "He continueth ever." Says ver. 25, "He ever liveth." Says ver. 28 "The Son, who is consecrated for evermore." In this chapter it is clearly and repeatedly "witnessed that He liveth."

The whole epistle is full of the same witness. The living Christ is the *rationale* of the superb treatise. The Old Testament is one great implication of the living Christ. The highest criticism of those ancient writings is that which discovers the Saviour as their centre and soul.

How Christ Himself witnessed to His own eternal life! Read two of His testimonies: "Henceforth ye shall see the Son of man sitting at the right hand of power, and coming in the clouds of heaven" (Matt. xxvi. 64). "Lo, I am with you always" ("all the days"), "even unto the end of the world" (Matt. xxviii. 20).

Every epistle of the New Testament bears distinct witness that He liveth, whilst the Apocalypse is a drama whose whole idea is to illustrate this vital fact. "I am the living One" is the voice of the mysterious Book.

Our Bibles should be dear to us, if only for their witness that Jesus liveth. I should not be assured that I have a living Lord had I not the Scripture testimony. My consciousness would not suffice without my Bible. My Bible is the firm foundation of my consciousness.   When hope is faint it gleams brightly again by the searching of the Scriptures.   Incalculable our indebtedness to the word of God—it is the earliest and most reassuring witness that Christ Jesus liveth.

If the living Christ be unrealized is not the explanation to be found in our neglected Bible ? The humble and studious Bible-reader has no doubt of the fact that He liveth.   Be sure that your apprehension of the living Saviour depends primarily and constantly upon your study of the Scriptures.   Keep close to your Bible, and it will keep you close to the living Christ.   The prevalent neglect of Bible-study by the mass of Christians is the secret of the dim witness they have of the ever-living One.   Precious witness-bearing word ! To company with it is to have the light of life !

II. THE BLESSING CHRIST IMPARTS IS WITNESS THAT HE LIVETH.

Our mystical writer regards Melchisedec's blessing as still in force.   " He whose genealogy is not counted from them—hath blessed him that hath the promises " (ver. 6, R.V).   The tense of the verb is the perfect and suggests permanence.   The blessing abides in all its early and tranquil force. The blessing of men is a priestly function, and the permanence of the benediction implies the permanence of the priesthood.

But it is only typically that Melchisedec's blessing abides. Christ actually blesses now. His priestly blessings are a present fact. Men receive blessings which can only come from Him. He alone promised to bestow them. He only does bestow them. That he gives blessing is witness that He liveth. What *words* of blessing Jesus gives! Full often He speaks immediately to the receptive soul. "It is the voice of my Beloved," the believing spirit jubilantly cries. The last earth saw of the departing Saviour was a vision of benediction. "While He blessed them He parted from them." And He has been speaking blessing upon His servants ever since. He thus sweetly speaks to-day. It is the unanimous avowal of Christian believers that the voice of Jesus sounds in their hearts. "It is witnessed" thus "that He liveth." He speaks to me, and I, hearing His voice, know that He lives.

Often He speaks to His people by the voice of men. The voices of His prophets are His voice. The Christian preacher is the voice of a voice. Any profit there ever is in a human ministry is wholly and solely due to its being

the channel of Jesus's words. Most blessed it is
to catch the voice of the Lord through human
tones. Lord, speak through Thy speakers!

Nor does the living Christ only speak blessing
by the voice of man, but also by books, and
song, and picture, and by other media. The
Saviour's voice comes to us through many in-
struments and oft as we hear it, howsoever it
cometh, we have witness that He liveth. Does
Jesus continually speak to you? And by all
means and ministries? Do you know His voice?
Then you need no further witness that He liveth.

But Christ's *deeds* of blessing confirm the
gracious and sustaining witness. Who bestows
the good things He is wont to bestow? Truly
there is none like unto Him. He gives pardon
to the trustful soul. He imparts comfort to the
sorrowful. He inspires with strength the weak
and weary. He creates sweet fellowship between
believers and the Father and Himself. Moreover, He unites in fellowship, deep and abiding,
all souls that obey their Lord. He thrills his
trusting ones with joy unspeakable and full of
glory. These blessings and others like unto them
are Christ's gifts. We know we possess them.
Of whom come they but of Him? Then these
delightsome blessings are witness that He liveth.

Do you enjoy these gracious gifts? Are you ever asking Christ's words of blessing and His works of blessing? We have not, because we ask not, or because we ask amiss. We should be always desiring and looking for these blessings. When Andrew Bonar saw his children pass his study window he gave them something to add to their happiness on their walk, and he quaintly wrote in his journal: " I urged this with the Lord, that He would see me passing and throw me some blessing." Let us all constantly urge this with the Lord. They who long for Christ's blessings shall receive them.

It is possible, however, to receive blessings and not accredit their divine source. Do you realize the living Christ in His blessings? or do the very blessings hide the Blesser from your eyes? Let all the blessings of grace be evidences to you of the living Lord. Trace Him and adore Him in His benefactions. They who see the Saviour in all gifts of grace need no persuasion that He liveth. He *does*, therefore He is.

III. THE WORSHIP WHICH IS OFFERED THROUGH AND TO CHRIST IS WITNESS THAT HE LIVETH.

Worship was offered to God through Melchisedec.

Tithes were received by the priest-king from
Abraham. In the mystical view of the holy
scribe Melchisedec still receives tithes; "he
receiveth them." Melchisedec is represented as
living and receiving in God's behalf the worship
which tithe-giving implies.

Now the worship offered this day and continually through Christ is a powerful witness to
His being the living Christ. Worship so offered
is right effectual—of this there is abundant witness. Therefore worship presented through such
a Mediator is witness that the Mediator lives.
Would men worship through a dead Mediator?
Only a living Mediator is a Mediator. There is
a most impressive testimony to the living Christ
in the presentation of worship through Him.
Christians invariably pray in His name. Their
sole hope of being heard lies in the name they
plead. They *are* heard. Then He liveth! Oft
as I plead in Christ's name I witness that He
liveth. I wing my prayers with this—"for Christ's
sake." Ever as I do so I have confirmation of
Christ as living. Assure your heart by this : He
lives, else to worship in His name were fatuous
indeed.

But we not only pay worship *through* Him, we
offer worship *to* Him. We go further far than

Abraham went with Melchisedec. He to us is God. We would not pray through Him if we could not pray to Him. An undivine mediator is no mediator.

All over Christendom Christ is worshipped. The first Christians worshipped Him as God. It is the earliest instinct of the Christian to cry, "My Lord and my God," to Jesus Christ. The heart is the true theologian, and the believing heart must worship Christ. What an irony is the worship of Christ if He be not alive! You cannot in any real or deep sense of the word worship a dead Being. The worship the generations give to Christ is witness that through the eddying ages He liveth. Every act of worship paid to the Saviour in public or in private is a testimony to the fact that He is alive. This is the essential implication of all Christian worship. We do well to confirm ourselves in the living Christ whenever we worship Him. Regard all worship as attestation of the living One. When your faith is low and love grows cold, give yourself to the worship of your Saviour, and He will witness to you as you worship that He liveth. Worship is a great apologetic. They lose an argument who are negligent of worship. Not the least of the reflex benefits of worship is the confirmation of our faith. We adore the Lord and the Lord reveals Himself. As we sing and pray and hear the God-commanded word, "It is witnessed that He liveth." Worship if you would be sure of the living Christ! Worship is a reviving tonic for a doubtful mind.

Do we habituate ourselves to realize the living Christ in worship? "Oh, come let us worship and bow down," and whilst we thus adore Jesus Himself will appear in the midst of us, a central glory, a dawning heaven.

IV. By the Oblations Given to Christ it is Witnessed that He Liveth.

Melchisedec was such that unto him "even the patriarch Abraham gave a tenth out of the chief spoils" (ver. 4, R.V.). The idea is that Abraham gave of the best of the spoils to that great personality who figuratively liveth still.

But what were the gifts lavished on Melchisedec compared with the offerings men gave to Christ? Given the best and holiest, the patriarchs of the later times, give the best of the spoils to Him. Who receives such gifts as does Jesus Christ? By so much it is witnessed that He liveth. Can the Christian consciousness be invariably deceived? It is unthinkable. Then the quantity and quality of the oblations dedicated to Christ powerfully witness to Him as the living One. Men give their best to Christ. The best give their very best to Him and deem it all unworthy. This they do quite voluntarily. All true sacrifices to Him are free-will offerings. The best of the spoils His servants gladly bestow on Him. They crown Him Lord of all. They speak of Him as peerless in strength and beauty. Language fails to describe His excellency. Christ's saints see Him to be so transcendent that they have none in heaven but Him, and none upon earth do they desire beside Him. So do Christian souls delight in the Lord that bought them that they cry, "Too much to Thee I cannot give." They will offer nothing to Him but "the chief spoils." Their grateful love deviseth liberal things, and by liberal things it stands. Christians glory to give Christ what costs them much. Burnt offerings without cost they utterly abhor, nor will they be constrained to offer such. Dr. A. J. Gordon, referring to a Christian undertaking in which he was deeply interested, said, "So far the effort has not paid financially, but, what is better, it has cost." Noble word! It is always better in Christ's service that things should cost than that they should pay. Oh the pure delight Christ's people have in offering to Him their best! When I see, the world over, the Saviour's disciples gladly giving Him their chiefest spoils I say, "It is witnessed that He liveth." Only a living Saviour could evoke such oblations. Examine that witness and its weight will increasingly impress you. Read the stirring tale of modern Christian chivalry. Ascertain what men and women have given up to Christ. And you will exclaim with tears of joy and gratitude, "It is witnessed that He liveth." Do you give your best to Christ? If so you are witnessing to all beholders that Christ liveth. Your sacrifices are testimonies. Your deeds are convincing arguments. Blessed are they who so testify amid a sinful age.

V. THE SUSTENANCE CHRIST AFFORDS IS WITNESS THAT HE LIVETH.

Melchisedec, who typically liveth for ever, " brought forth bread and wine " to the exhausted warrior-patriarch as he returned victorious from the scene of strife. (Gen. xiv. 8.)

Jesus Christ, the true Melchisedec, is wont to meet all His weary ones and refresh them. Never do His servants lack support, especially in life's strenuous hours. Does not Christ sustain His people? He gives them temporal food. He visits

them in their necessity and tenderly says,
"Children, have ye any meat?" He cares about
common things. He is not remote from
mundane cares. He is solicitous concerning our
"meat." Christ often comes into our life by the
temporal door. We know Him as He breaks
bread for our hungry bodies. Our Melchisedec
meets His servants in their spent moments, and
refreshes them with right invigorating refreshment,
till they sing, "Bless the Lord, O my soul . . . who
satisfieth thy mouth with good things, so that
thy youth is renewed like the eagle's." Many and
many a time has the sustenance wherewith He
has replenished our physical frame witnessed to
us that Christ Jesus liveth. He has "all authority"
on earth. He is heir of all things, and has already
received His inheritance. Perhaps we all too
little realize "the cosmical significance of Christ."
He rules the all things that were made by Him.
And He delights to feed His people with the
bread of this life.

Christ restores our souls with yet richer sustenance. Continually He meets us when we are
faint with life's struggles and brings forth bread
and wine. He spreads a table in the wilderness,
where most a table is required. He nourishes
us with sacramental food. We should utterly

faint did not our Saviour rally us with heavenly fare. This is a commonplace of Christian experience, but it is a splendid commonplace. Is it a reality to you? You often have to slaughter the kings, and it depletes you quite. Weary and exhausted, does your Melchisedec not bring forth bread and wine? Yes, often you taste and see how gracious the Lord is. He appears just when your need is sorest. His set time is the time of need. Our weakness attracts Him. Our sadness lures Him.

We find such sustenance a witness that He liveth. I know and am persuaded that Jesus lives, for He upholds me in the fainting hour. My foot had slipped if He had not helped me; when, hungry and thirsty, my soul fainted in me, He brought forth His bread and wine. Verily He liveth! We need no added witness. Only yesterday and again to-day, when I was returning from the slaughter of the kings, Christ Jesus met me with bread and wine. "It is witnessed that He liveth."

VI. By the Quality of His Character it is Witnessed that He Liveth.

This also is part of the inspired argument in the memorable chapter before us. In ver. 4 we

read, "Now consider how great this man was"—
then elements of his greatness are produced.
"Consider" means "spiritually contemplate."
And the greatness referred to is moral greatness.
But all the while the antitype is blended with
the type. Mystically speaking, Melchisedec was
too great morally for him to die, No death of
this morally great man is recorded.

When we address ourselves to Christ Jesus,
we are compelled to say, "Consider how great
this man was." Nay! Not "was." So great an
one could not die in any final sense. "It is
witnessed that He liveth." Such a Being *must*
live eternally. The character of Christ argues,
and irresistibly argues. His immortality. Nothing
so effectually witnesses that He liveth as does
the character of Christ. The Holy One *cannot*
see corruption. The argumentative value of
Christ's character is incalculable. The Christ
of God can never die. He liveth! We realize
the witness of His peerless character. Lord
Tennyson said, "The spiritual character of Christ
is more wonderful than the greatest miracle."
And so wonderful a character suggests "the power
of an endless life." Being what He was, Christ
must be for ever such. Ponder Christ's incomparable character. Ask that the Spirit may make

it glorious in your eyes, so will the ever-living Christ be a grand reality to you. Such a flower can never fade.

By many other elements is it witnessed that Christ liveth, but we purposely limit ourselves to those which are suggested by Melchisedec, Christ's great type. These constitute a powerful testimony to the living Christ. Such a witness gives light to the mind and rest to the heart.

Is the living Christ a great and bright reality to us? Oh, never cease to strive in prayer that this may be so. If the living Christ be vividly realized by the Churches, great and apostolic will be their triumphs in these evening hours of time.

I will close by reminding you of the manner by which the living Christ became a potent reality to that great preacher, Dr. R. W. Dale. It was out of this rapturous experience he came to write his kindling book, "The Living Christ." He was writing an Easter sermon, and when halfway through, the thought of the risen Lord broke in upon him as it had never done before. "'Christ is alive,' I said to myself; 'alive!' and then I paused. 'Alive!' and then I paused again; 'Alive! Can that really be true? living as really as I myself am?' I got up and walked

about repeating, 'Christ is living ! Christ is living !'
At first it seemed strange and hardly true, but
at last it came upon me as a burst of sudden
glory ; yes, Christ is living. It was to me a new
discovery. I thought that all along I had believed
it ; but not until that moment did I feel sure
about it. I then said, 'My people shall know
it ; I shall preach about it again and again until
they believe it as I do now.'" For months
afterwards, and in every sermon, the living Christ
was his one great theme, and there and then
began the custom of singing in Carr's Lane
on every Sunday morning an Easter hymn.

When a friend expressed surprise at hearing
an Easter hymn sung there one November
morning, Dr. Dale said, "I want my people to
get hold of the glorious fact that Christ is alive,
and to rejoice over it, and Sunday, you know,
is the day on which Christ left the dead."

May we all realize as did Dr. Dale that "it
is witnessed that He liveth"!

VIII

THE INCOMPARABLENESS OF CHRIST

" What is thy Beloved more than another beloved, O thou fairest among women? What is thy Beloved more than another beloved, that thou dost so charge us ? "—SOL. SONG v. 9.

ONE of the greatest of Christian teachers essayed to answer that inquiry. And he did so with consummate success. John Owen's glorious book on "The Glory of Christ" is a sublime response to the appeal before us. The great work was expressly intended to solve the problem and it is undoubtedly a most intellectual and spiritual solution. John Owen begins his immortal book by saying, " We shall endeavour an answer unto the inquiry made unto the spouse by the daughters of Jerusalem." Let me earnestly commend Owen on " The Glory of Christ " as the grandest purely human attempt to answer the urgent inquiry to which I now call your thoughts.

I accept with increasing acceptation the spiritual interpretation of the Song of Songs. To me this song is full of Christ. Here He hides me in the secret of His presence as scarcely otherwhere in Holy Scripture. And the theme with which my text burns and glows is the incomparableness of Christ.

I do not stay to discuss whether the question is to be supposed as asked seriously or ironically. I prefer to think of it as intended seriously ; but be it addressed seriously or flippantly, let our reply be full of glad solemnity.

" What is thy Beloved more than another beloved ? " Wherein is Christ incomparable ? Many replies might be adduced. I simply select four items which are shrined in the inquiry itself. Thus in a very real and inspiring sense the question shall be its own answer.

I. CHRIST IS INCOMPARABLE IN THE IN-QUIRIES HE EXCITES.

There must be something in our Beloved that is more than another beloved when such interrogatories are urged upon us. Why inquire so much about Him if there be nothing transcendent in Him ? Why such interest if there be in Him no glory that excelleth ? Commonplaceness does not arrest attention. Mediocrity does not challenge comparison. Ordinary personalities do not nor-

mally create extraordinary excitement. But our
Beloved is much inquired about. He looms like
a great and lucent star upon the wondering eyes
of multitudes in many lands. Christ's people are
always being inquired of concerning their Beloved.
Never was this more markedly so than to-day.
The students of comparative religions, the man
in the street, the toiling masses, the literary
and philosophic and scientific *élite*, the moralists
—all are crying, " What is thy Beloved more than
another beloved, O thou fairest among women ?
What is thy Beloved more than another beloved,
that thou dost so charge us ? "

The world, man considered as apart from God,
is urging this inquiry in unprecedented degree.
Certainly Jesus has touched the world's imagination ; happily also He has touched its conscience,
The world is gone after Him. All men in some
sense seek Him. As when He was here and
much more abundantly, He cannot be hid. No
figure of history or contemporary life arrests
attention as does Jesus Christ. Account for the
fact as we may, the hard fact remains. The world
is intensely interested in the Saviour. He has
somehow gripped the world's heart. He has been
lifted up, and through the reluctant centuries He
is drawing all men unto Him.

No popular novel sells like one which presents a vision of Christ. Any man in any sphere who has a living word about Christ to speak is sure of a hearing. Certainly in this Jesus Christ is incomparable. He is at least so far "more than another beloved."

What an inquiry He arouses among His own people! How apt they are to appeal either to other with grateful adoration of their Lord, and say, "What is thy Beloved more than another beloved, O thou fairest among women?" The Christian believer is simply entranced with Christ. The Song of Songs has no love-language too sweet for the lips of the spirit-filled Christian. Dull tepid souls that have never been baptized with the Holy Ghost and with fire may deprecate the ardours of the holy song. But it is none too rapturous for those who know their Lord. So intensely does Christ fill all things to His saints that the world calls it an infatuation. No! It is an inspiration! Christ ravishes the hearts of His Church. He is precious beyond all preciousness to them that believe. They never weary of studying Him. He is all and in all to them. He is the last because He was the first, and He is the first because He will be the last. Christ's servants love no books like those which unfold

His glories. They delight in the Bible chiefly because it pours light on His altogether lovely form. They love no society save that in which He is glorified. To talk of Him, to write of Him, this is their dearest pursuit. Such excitation of such inquiry is unique. None other ever awakened such keen enthusiastic interest as He. Truly He is in this regard "more than another beloved."

The inquiry concerning Christ is so reiterated. Twice in this one verse is the question urged. The circumstance is very suggestive. How perpetually is the problem of the Saviour raised! Century succeeds century, but to witness the renewal of inquiries about the Son of the Blessed. The form of the questioning changes, but the subject is ever the same. The generations have their own vocabulary, and outlook, and emphasis, but their inquiries are concerning one Jesus. Not once nor twice is the cry heard. The ages are one in the pressure of this appeal. But little in common do the years present to our view, but in their interest in Jesus they manifest a strange and pathetic and gladdening identity. How is this to be accounted for? If Christ be incomparable in this, may it not be that He is incomparable in all things?

His transcendency is practically assumed in the inquiries we hear. It is all but so in our text. "What is thy Beloved *more than* another beloved? What is thy Beloved *more than* another beloved?" Neither the world nor the Church is content to assume Christ's mere equality with others, the question involves His supremacy. The concessions which the general inquiry about Christ make are singularly instructive. His superiority is admitted, only the philosophy of it is discussed. This in itself is an argument. Why is it assumed that Christ is "more than" others? Surely the assumption is an argument. The concession is an unconscious apologetic. As for Christ's servants, the "more than" is their argumentative starting-point. This is their first axiom. They crown Him "Lord *of all.*" Their glowing assumption is that Christ is "*more than* another beloved." This is the basal music of their noblest songs.

The repeated inquiry in this text of mine arises from the testimony the lover has borne to the Beloved. The Beloved has so captivated the bride that she has made no secret of her love. She has sung the praises of her Beloved everywhere. On the astonished ears of the passers by her love-songs have fallen. She has been so positively intoxicated with love that she could not be silent about the absorbing theme. And her reiterated testimony has aroused reiterated inquiry. Thank God, we may attribute much of the inquiry about Christ to the witness His people have given! Would God we could credit it still more completely to that agency! Christian testimony has not been withheld from Christ. The world owes much to such testimony. If believers had been dumb dogs the interest in the Saviour would never have been what it is. Christian witness-bearing has stimulated the world's interest. What have you, my Christian friend, done in this direction? Whose mind have you directed inquiringly towards Jesus? Do you sing your Beloved's praises? If in your neighbourhood there be a decadent interest in Christ, perchance your restrained testimony may explain the untoward state of things. Speak up for thy Saviour, O man, for whom He has done so great things! Silence may be treachery. Dumbness may be denial. Rouse the world by thy witnessing! Perchance they shall seek after Him if thou chant His praise!

There is a great and satisfying reply to all inquiry about Jesus the Saviour. Do they ask, "What is thy Beloved more than another beloved?" In glad tones the bride describes

the Beloved's surpassing charms. The verses
which follow are the reply to the query of the
text. There is a definite, detailed, and convincing answer to the inquiries concerning Jesus.
Never let us check inquiry. Never depreciate
or dread it. We have a glorious and substantial
reason for the hope that is in us. Christ is a
satisfying portion.

Do *you* inquire about the Saviour? Do you
ask as foe or friend? As an outsider or as
His beloved? Is it so that you are ever inquiring
after Him? Then be assured your solicitude
is a tribute to His incomparableness. It is a
crown upon His much-crowned brow.

II. CHRIST IS INCOMPARABLE IN THE LOVE
HE EVOKES.

Note the epithet, "thy Beloved." Note that
it is twice repeated. Note also that it is often
used in this Book. One of the designations the
bride applies is this, "Him whom my soul loveth."
Those who inquire concerning her Beloved, see
how she loves Him. "Beloved" is the term
by which they speak of Him. There is no
designation by which Christ can be more suitably
spoken of. Christ is dearly loved of His people.
They love Him with a love passing the love

of women. "What is thy Beloved more than another beloved?" Why, He is incomparable in creating such warmth of love in His lovers' hearts! Christ draws out love as none other can. He dominates love as He dominates everything. In nothing is Christ's incomparableness seen more clearly than in this. Others evoke love; there are many beloveds; but this Beloved is "more than another beloved," for none lay up such wealth of love as He. This is His supremacy. As Napoleon said, "Jesus alone founded His empire upon love." And so His empire outlasts all other empires and outlasts the universe. There is no rival to the love Christ institutes in a believing heart. For the sake of that love all other loves have been surrendered. In the strength of that love what deeds of prowess have been achieved! How that love has absorbed the souls of men! Unquestionably it has been the supreme motive force of the Christian centuries. Men have stood amazed with strong amazement in presence of that love. It has put to silence the ignorance of foolish men. When other religious leaders can inspire such love they may claim to be the rivals of Jesus, and not till then. The love of the bride was intense. Oh, how she yearned over and gloried in her Beloved!

She had no tranquillity in his absence. Life lost its colour, and all its glory was in eclipse when He was gone. She was often "sick of love," and no flagons could stay her, no apples comfort her. Her Beloved was her other and better self. Thus it has been with many a Christian towards the Lord. "This is my Beloved" has been the watchword of the life. The night was as day if He were near by. The radiant morn was black with sevenfold gloom if He were wanting. Have *we* an intense love to Christ? Do we so fervently love Him that the world is made to feel how incomparable Christ is by reason of the love He has evoked from us? A great love to Christ draws observers Christward.

The love of the bride was manifest to everyone. They could not speak of Him save as "thy Beloved." It was patent to all that His love possessed her whole. She blushed not to own it on every hand. She would have blushed to be silent about it. She would have deemed reticence to be disloyalty. That is the true temper of life. Make it manifest that Jesus has taken possession of your heart. Speak and act as those who desire that all should know how entirely you love your Beloved. These times call for pronounced love to Jesus. False

delicacy may be true apostasy. Confess your
ardently grateful love to Him, to whom your
more than all you owe. The evangelicals often
used to ask men and women if they loved Jesus.
We too should be urgent on this point. "If
any man love not the Lord Jesus Christ let him
be anathema." Samuel Rutherford delighted to
discourse on "the loveliness of Christ." Be
this our constant theme. Pray God we have
eyes to see that loveliness and hearts to love it
fervently. O Spirit of God, make Christ Jesus
so lovely in our eyes that henceforth we shall
love Him as He loves us!

III. CHRIST IS INCOMPARABLE IN THE BEAUTY
OF THOSE WHO FOLLOW HIM.

The loveliness of the bride appeals to those who
inquire of her and they exclaim, "O thou fairest
among women." Previously she has been so
addressed (Ch. i. 8), and subsequently she is again
similarly addressed (Ch. vi. 1). Indeed, it was
largely by reason of her loveliness that bystanders
and friends challenged her concerning her Beloved.
They felt that He must be glorious after whom
so beautiful a being followed. "O thou fairest
among women."

And it is generally the beauty of Christ's

followers which leads men and women to inquire after Him. He beautifies His lovers. His beauty is upon them. Far more often than by intellectual arguments the loveliness of the Christian draws to Christ. The evangelistic influence of a lovely soul is great beyond compare. Beautiful lives constrain men to seek the Lord who is the source of beauty.

Every true Christian is exceeding fair. None of the earthborn race are so fair. Beholding as in a mirror the glory of the Lord, they are changed into the same image. They grow fairer with the years ; from glory to glory they pass in lovely progressiveness.

Some saints have received a surpassing loveliness. They have had communicated to them a singular charm. "O thou fairest among women," has the astonished world exclaimed. A study of such lives is a means of grace of highest quality. None can know them without desiring to know their Lord.

These beautiful followers of Jesus are supremely fair in all eyes but their own. They are blind to their own beauty. Perfect loveliness is ever unconscious of itself. The fairer a companion of Jesus becomes the less fair does that soul realize itself to be. "Saints are lovely in *His* sight." Jesus delights in the grace He Himself has given.

He joys to behold His own loveliness reflected in lovely souls. The world, often in spite of itself, is constrained to say, "O thou fairest among women." And it is drawn to thoughts of the Saviour by the vision of beauty it beholds in the followers of the Saviour.

O companions of the Christ, seek loveliness of soul! Be as an ideal of fair beauty among the sons and daughters of men! Except you are as "the fairest among women," the world will not turn to the one Saviour. Pray without ceasing that your Lord's beauty may be upon you. Thus your loveliness will attract the world towards Him who has made your life sublime.

"What is thy Beloved more than another beloved?" Here is an answer, ready and adequate. None have such followers as He. He makes His servants beautiful. The fairest are they who do His bidding. It is in the train of Jesus earth's loveliest are found. Consider this, and seek the Lord, that your lives may of Him be made beautiful with a beauty on whose fadeless bloom time cannot breathe.

IV. CHRIST IS INCOMPARABLE IN THE EARNESTNESS WHICH HE INSPIRES.

"What is thy Beloved more than another

beloved, O thou fairest among women? What is thy Beloved more than another beloved, *that thou dost so charge us?*"

Christ's follower is represented by those around her as charging them. The R.V. reads it "that thou dost so adjure us." Adjuration is an intense and solemn charge. Joshua adjured the people not to rebuild Jericho. The High Priest adjured Jesus to tell if He were the Christ.

This is typical of Christ's followers—they adjure the world and they adjure one another. What zeal Christ kindles in His people! Who creates such an earnest following as our Beloved does? No beloved is comparable to Him in this. The solemn fervour of His people attests His worth.

Napoleon was impressed with the earnestness Christ inspires in Christians. He said, " Millions would die for Him." It is gloriously true. Earnestness not only expresses itself in Christian speech but in Christian act. What deeds sacrificially zealous Christ's people do for Him! A missionary mother parting with her children exclaimed, " O Saviour, I do this for Thee." For none other would she have done it! The Christian's intensity of devotion to Christ knows no parallel.

But the particular type of earnestness to which

the text refers is that of earnest admonition to others. We must adjure men if we follow Christ. We are called, and by grace compelled, to plead concerning Christ with those around us, especially with those who know Him not. Every Christian is a home-missionary in virtue of being a Christian. He must "adjure." A Christian has been described as "a man to whom the Lord has *entrusted* his fellows." We are bound to realize our solemn responsibility. We are our brother's keeper. His blood will be required at our hands. Take care that earnestly and lovingly and continually you "charge" those with whom you are associated. Charge them that there is no blessedness but in Christ. Charge them that He died to save a lost world. Charge them that except they repentantly accept Christ they shall perish. We need constantly to reinforce our evangelistic zeal. So easily the fervent heat dies down! Is there not more than a danger that we fail to "charge" the world? "Christians should be troublesome to the world," says Mr. Spurgeon. But are we so in these days? More than once in this spiritual song the Church is depicted as "terrible." I fear we seldom terrify the world to-day. Spirit of the Lord, arouse us, that when the voice of our Beloved is heard in Second Advent awfulness, we may be manifested as faithful evangelists who have charged men in the Lord's behalf!

So in the terms of the inquiry we have found answer to the enquiry. Our Beloved is "more than another beloved." None are so inquired after. None are so loved. None have followers marked by such exceeding beauty. None inspire such earnestness in their disciples.

Are you satisfied that your Beloved is "more than another beloved"?

Is He "the chiefest among ten thousand" to you? Is He "altogether lovely" in your gladdened vision?

So love and serve the Christ, the Saviour of the world, that on every side men shall inquire of you, "Whither is thy Beloved gone, O thou fairest among women? Whither is thy Beloved turned aside? that we may seek Him with thee."

IX

THE INDWELLING CHRIST

"Christ in you, the hope of glory."—Col. i. 27.

THIS great saying is a gem from a casket of gems. How wonderfully rich is this first chapter of Colossians! The cabinet is close-packed with pearls. More than once in his deeply suggestive journal Dr. Chalmers says, "Much delighted with the first chapter of Colossians." Have you re-read it recently? I pray you do so, and you will make a similar entry concerning this august chapter in your journal.

There is no wealthier word in the chapter than this text of mine. "Christ in you, the hope of glory." Spurgeon, whose eye could penetrate the depths, annotated it thus: "The words read like a whole body of divinity condensed into a line." Such indeed they are. Let us seek to ascertain somewhat of this so-condensed body of divinity.

I. This is the Central Fact of Christianity. "Christ in you."

Would you call this the *central* fact of Christian
doctrine and life? Yes. Would you not rather
say that the central fact is expressed in this
formula, "Christ for you"? No. Christ for us
is a fundamental formula. It is the basal doctrine
of Christianity. But I would not describe it as
the central thesis. Because Christ is only *for* us
that He may be *in* us. Christ's indwelling is the
goal and end of redemption. He died and rose
and ascended and intercedes for us in order that
He may dwell in us. And Christ is for us in
vain if He be not *in* us. So that, increasingly
as I meditate, I affirm that "Christ in you" is
the very core of the experimental theology of
Christianity.

But how can Christ be in us? I thought He
was in heaven: throned in glory everlasting. So
He is, yet is He in us. As to the body He is
on the throne of the Highest. The loving man
rules the courts of heaven. But he is in us as
to His Spirit. Being God He is "omnipresent."
Easy to drop that theological term! But who
can define it adequately or describe it vividly?
God is present everywhere at the same time. A

truth this which is beyond the intellectual range, but were it not, God would be unbelievable. None could credit a God they could comprehend.

But the fact, romantic and transcendent, remains though we cannot understand it. We believe where we cannot prove. Christ is " illimitable God," and so, unlike mere man, His Spirit is universal. He is seated on heaven's most splendid throne, yet He is " in you." He has two homes, one glorious beyond compare, the other mean and inadequate—the heaven of heavens and the trustful heart.

Accepting the wonderful fact, by what instrument on the human side does He come to dwell in man? Let Paul, the great preacher of Christian mysticism, tell us. One of Paul's prayers was "that Christ may dwell in your heart *by faith.*" It is through that little unimposing door He enters human personalities. " Christ in *you* :" —the "you" is not the clever, the intellectual, the ecclesiastical, the self-satisfied. The "you" is the believing, the trustful, the reliant. O wonderfullest of condescension! He whom throngs of angels adore dwells in the heart that trusts Him! Verily this is Christianity's sublimest doctrine, its coronating experience, its transcendental fact.

"Christ in you." What a *romantic* fact is this! Evangelicalism is sometimes derided as unpoetic, unromantic, a hard iron system of thought. They who have so represented it have grossly caricatured it. Evangelicalism, rightly conceived, is full of romance, poetry, idealism. "Christ in you" is so splendid a concept that one feels its very splendour to be a witness to its veracity. The sublimest things, depend upon it, are the truest. On Truth's clear brow shine many crowns. "Christ in you." This is the *sanctifying principle* of life. Sad it is that so many of the most earnest souls are looking in the wrong direction for sanctification. It cometh not along any path outside of us. It journeyeth by the inward way. It is by the yielding up of the nature to the indwelling Christ that true holiness is achieved. Christ is in you, O believer! Let Him have full play with you! And the indwelling Christ will transform without effacing your personality. "Let us be borne on to perfection."

"Christ in you." This is the *regal element* in the Christian character. If He dwell in me, my nature becomes His palace, and He, my King, reigns there with unchallenged rule. He does His own sweet will therein. It is mine to obey Him. My King commands within me, and I delight to do His will. "Christ in you." This is the *evidential* power. Christ is the true "inward light." The Christian does not depend so much on arguments without as on illumination within The indwelling Christ witnesses truth to me and rejects error. Many an else most difficult religious problem is easily solved if Christ dwell in us. He conducts a teaching ministry within us. He settles many a point of criticism, biblical and theological. "We shall not full direction need" if Christ be in us. The indwelling Christ authenticates the things of God to our intellect and heart and conscience.

"Christ in you." Here is the *secret of self-reverence!* If my body be His shrine can I desecrate that shrine? All wrong done to the body or to any part of human personality is sacrilege. One in whom Christ dwells must reverence himself. Such cannot be merely self-respecting, they will be self-reverential. Not self-conceited, but self-awed! Herein is the explanation of the dignity which graces many of the humblest Christians. We not seldom wonder at the refinement of spirit and of manner manifested by some who are poor and unschooled. We call it "native refinement." But it is not "native." It springs from the consciousness of

Christ mystical. Lowly people are noble-mannered when Christ is homed in their hearts. •We shall revere ourselves with evangelical reverence if Christ be in us of a truth.

"Christ in you." This is the *fount of sweetest comfort.* What soothes amid sorrow like the consciousness of the indwelling Christ? This is a pure deep fount of consolation in the heart, more refreshing far than the most sparkling fountain by the way. How would some of you sustain the heavy burdens of life save for Christ being in you? In the extremes of pain and woe what has upheld you but this? What supported you on the sad journey to the cemetery, and on the sadder journey home again, excepting this alone —"Christ in you"? This glowing centre of Christian experience is ardent consolation.

Every way, how great, how sublimely helpful is this great fact of our faith. O blest experience. My friends, do you know it? Transcending definition, it does not transcend experience. Have you entered into the treasures of this ineffable indwelling? "Christ in you." Are you one of that "you"? Entreat the living Lord Christ this very moment to enter your heart. Let that heart be His "mean but constant home." Say with repentant trustfulness, "Come in, my

Lord, come in." And He will be gracious to accept your heart's hospitality. Nor will He ever rest till He hath changed your nature. He will erewhile transfigure your very flesh. Christ will live in you.

Paul describes this doctrine of the indwelling Christ as a *mystery*. He does so in the verse of which my text is a part. He also does so in the previous verse. " Ah," says one, " it is indeed a mystery." But are you quite sure that what Paul meant by the word is identical with our present-day meaning? It is, in fact, entirely different. The word "mystery" is an example of words which through the centuries have all but revolutionized their meaning. The word " mystery" meant on Paul's lips almost the opposite of what it means in modern speech. A very profitable Bible-study might be made of the New Testament use of this word. Paul borrowed the term from contemporary religions. They made much of their " mysteries." By a " mystery" they indicated a truth, or a rite which was reserved only for the select circle of the initiated. It was a something which was not generally known, but was understood only of those who had learned the secret. It was that which could only be known by a special revelation. Now Paul frequently

gives that suggestive word a Christian application.
And he always uses it, not to suggest mysterious-
ness in our modern sense, but a something which
can only be known by divine revelation.   A
"mystery," with Paul, is a truth or experience
divinely revealed.   The heathen religionists said,
" Our mysteries can only be known by the favoured
few who have been initiated."   Paul exclaimed
with brimming soul and tuneful voice, " Our
mysteries may be known by all who will submit
to the obedience of faith.   *All* may be initiated.
Our secret is revealed."

Now read Paul's phrase as applied to the
doctrine of the indwelling Christ, " This mystery
among the Gentiles; which is Christ in you."
This is a "mystery," a secret which only the
initiated know.   But all may know it.   All shall
know it if they will but believe.

Oh how sublime is this " mystery."   They know
it not who have not faith.   Have *you* learned
the secret?   Are *you* initiated?   Well may they
who are strangers to the "mystery" deride it
or ignore it, or pity us as visionaries and fanatics.
They know not the interior experience.   Genius
and ethicalism are alike naturally strangers to this
mystery.   Only faith knows the secret, has the
clue, knows the password, can ring out the con-

fident " Sesame." O my soul, come thou more and
ever more into this secret. Christianity is wholly
supernatural. Uninspired man never discovered
this splendid "mystery." "Christ in you" can
only be understood by those who through sovereign
grace have been admitted into the divine secret.
Paul speaks of the "mystery" of "Christ in you"
as having been *long hidden.* "Even the mystery
which hath been hid from all ages and generations"
(ver. 26, R.V.).

This is a pathetic and strange fact. In the
Old Testament ages and generations Christ was
perceived in the spirit of prophecy. But the
indwelling Christ was not realized. The noble
old-time saints who saw Christ's day did not see
the day of His indwelling. Why did God not
reveal the secret sooner? Why were the golden
gates of "this mystery" kept close-locked? Ah,
why? It is all but vain to ask. We can but fall
back upon the grand doctrine of the sovereignty
of God. He doeth what He pleaseth. He
speaketh and it is done. He doth not speak and
it is not done. But this we know, that God's
sovereignty is not capricious, not despotic. It
is the exercise of limitless and all-wise love. And
on that sovereignty we rest—it is our only rock
of refuge amid the inscrutable things of life.

Faith accepts the fact and patiently awaits the explanation.

The great teacher tells us also of this wonderful doctrine that *only Christian character can apprehend it.* He says, " But now (it) is made manifest to *His saints* (ver. 26). Christian believers are ever called "saints " in the New Testament. There is another word which has greatly and sadly changed its meaning. " Saints" are not in Scripture signification a special order of Christians. It is a general designation of Christ's consecrated ones. The indwelling of Christ is " made manifest to His saints." The genius of Christian experience is not intellectual but spiritual. Christian character clearly sees these secret sanctities. The " mystery " is not made manifest to scholarship as such, or to cleverness as such, or to morality as such, but to Christian believing. Is it made manifest to you? Then you are one of " His saints." Oh, test yourself by this golden and infallible standard.

Yet further. Paul avows that the experimental doctrine of the indwelling Christ is *exceeding precious.* He writes ecstatically of " the riches of the glory of this mystery (ver. 27). " Riches" have always a unique and spiritual connotation when spoken of by Paul. " Oh the wealth of this experience ! " he cries. " Glory " is one of Paul's great and favourite terms. He delights to pen the splendid word. How much he signifies by it we cannot fully divine. It suggests unspeakable splendour : joy unutterable : royalty beyond all dreaming. He declares that there is "glory" in the experience of "Christ in you." It is a present heaven. But he is not content to represent it as only "riches" or only "glory." He avers it to be both. "The riches of the glory of this mystery." It is wealthy and splendid. Its riches are glorious. Its glory is opulent.

And this language is not too exalted. Who can adequately set forth the rapture of the experience of the indwelling Christ? It defies all description. Its colours have no equivalent on any palette of earthly studio. It passeth knowledge. Do *you* know the inexpressible delight of this "mystery"? Blessed for ever with ever-accumulating blessedness are they who know in their daily experience this central fact of our holy faith. To them God has made known "what is the riches of the glory of this mystery."

II. This Central Christian Fact has a Notable Working.

I might illustrate from the context several impressive aspects of this truth. It could readily be shown that the indwelling Christ is *the secret of enduring suffering.* "*Now* I rejoice in my sufferings" (ver. 24, R.V.). For Christ's sake and for the Church's sake Paul bore a martyrdom of pain. And it was the indwelling Christ who upheld him as he traversed his thorny path.

The great verity is *the supreme idea and inspiration of the Christian ministry.* "Whereof I am made a minister, according to the dispensation of God, which is given to me for you, to fulfil the word of God ; *even* the mystery—" (vers. 25, 26). This truth is the final earthly fulfilment of the word of God. And this only gives a ministry true completeness. This alone is adequate inspiration for a noble Christian ministration.

The doctrine of the indwelling Christ *makes a universal appeal.* It is preached freely "among the Gentiles" (ver. 27). It is preachable always and everywhere. "Whom we preach," says St. Paul (ver. 28). And note his *clientèle !* Observe the repetitious—"every man." To all men everywhere is this glorious doctrine pertinent : all are capable of knowing this radiant "mystery."

But I desire specially to call your thought to the working of this truth which is adduced in my text itself. Paul declares it is "*the hope of glory.*"

That is the phase of the doctrine which seems

to loom brightly in the forefront of the Apostle's mind. There are those who would almost limit the "glory" to the present life. They conceive it to be the glory of ennobled Christian character in this world. And that is the true glory of men and of nations. But I cannot conceive that to be an adequate exposition. As Bishop Moule has pointed out, the term "hope" seems to point to the eternal future. It is of the "glory" which irradiates the world above that Paul is descanting. He is thinking, dreaming, singing of the illumination, and majesty, and ecstasy which awaits Christ's people when they have passed in Christ's presence and strength through the valley of the shadow of death. "Christ in you, the hope of glory."

The indwelling Christ is the hope of the glorious life of the world to come. And He is so in two ways.

(*a*) He is *the basis* of that blessed hope. We *know* there is "glory" beyond the evening shades of time because we have Christ in us as a present fact. The proof of heavenly bliss is the indwelling of Christ. The sweetness of this rapturous experience yieldeth proof of immortality. This is the crowning evidence of immortal bliss to a Christian believer. He values, more or less, all literary and argumentative proofs of the great beyond ; and the cumulative evidence is a moral demonstration. But to him the grandest argument is mystical ; it is drawn from his present consciousness of Christ in him. A man in whom Christ dwells cannot die eternally. Heaven, immortal heaven, must be the destiny of one whose breast is Jesus's shrine. "Christ in you" is the firm foundation of "the hope of glory." We do well as Christ's men and women ever to recur to this ground of all our hope. Perhaps we too much forget this in these days. O ye mortal men and women who have Christ in you, cease not to remember that this is "the hope of glory"! If Christ be "the strength of my heart," He will inevitably be my "portion for ever." Go back continually and gratefully upon this basal reason of the hope that is in us. Delight to reckon yourselves children of the resurrection because Christ is in you. You may have little aptitude or inclination for the evidential studies which enchain some, but here is an evidence verifiable every day, solid, impregnable—"Christ in you, the hope of glory." If I know the indweller I have infallible warranty for expecting "glory" when my pilgrim days are spent.

(β) The indwelling Christ is *the encouragement* of

the hope of glory. When Christ dwells in us we cherish that blessed hope. The lamp is burnished till its silver radiance charms all eyes and the sacred flame glows with fervent heat, which cheers and warms those who come nigh it. Wherever Christ dwells within the hope of glory is fostered. Say I to my soul, "Oh, what a blessed hope is thine." Say I to the Church, " Ye shall be counted worthy to attain that world." And I say it more and more emphatically as I know that Christ dwelleth in me and in them. My dear friend, if Christ be in you of a truth, the hope of glory must be very real. If you depend on anything else as the encouragement of that hope, the immortal gleam will fade, but this sense of indwelling Deity will keep it vivid. None can be sure of glory save by the indwelling of Christ. I do not say the hope will always be equable. Our very health and the changefulness of our circumstances will affect the degree of the rapture. But the hope will never ebb out if Christ be in us. Oh, encourage the unspeakable hope by cherishing the divine indwelling !

Now here is a test I may well apply to myself, whereby I may know if Christ is in me. Have I the hope of glory? Faintly, or dimly, have I the hope ? Am I assured that beyond the " dark

gate across the wild " there is " glory " for me,
even for me ?   Then assuredly Christ is in you.
The hope is proof of the indwelling, as the indwelling is evidence of the hope.

I sometimes surmise that the present generation of Christians does not encourage " the hope
of glory " as former generations did.   I trust
I am in error on this supposition, but it persists
with me.   Oh, if Christ be in us, the hope of glory
will be bright, living, and active.   Is it ?   Do
we often take Richard Baxter's advice, and walk
imaginatively through the golden streets where
soon we hope in the spiritual body to walk ?
If this holy habit be decadent I fear lest the
sense of " Christ in you " be decadent too.   God
forbid !

Oh, encourage, by reason of the indwelling Christ,
this hope of glory.   Be heaven and its felicities
very real to you.   Smile at the popular cant
against "otherworldliness."   A true otherworldliness
is creative of a true worldliness.   None are such
citizens of earth as they who joy to exclaim,
" Our citizenship is in heaven."   The realization
of the eternal bliss is necessary to the perfecting
of the saints in time.   " The hope of glory " is the
great sanctifying force.   Character is transfigured
here by the prospect of immortal joys.

Have you "the hope of glory"? You cannot have it except Christ be in you. Seek by simple, penitent, obedient faith to receive Christ into your heart, its most precious guest. Then you will delight to encourage "the hope of glory." You shall sing even at the grave, "It is better further on."

X

THE PRUDENCE OF CHRIST

"Behold, My servant shall deal prudently."—ISA. lii. 13.

IS not this an unfamiliar prophecy of Christ? A prophecy of Christ it most assuredly is. Have not many of us left this element out of our Christology? We think of Jesus Christ as the incarnate holiness, as love embodied, as the soul of sympathy. Of His power we often think. But do we frequently consider His prudence?

Frankly, we are inclined to doubt as to the prudence of Christ. He was wondrously heroic. He had an enthusiasm of self-sacrifice. He rushed to the outstretched arms of His cross. But we hesitate to describe Him as prudent. Yet this prophecy of my text is a fulfilled prophecy. Therefore our conception of Christ must be erroneous in this particular. What if we have a mistaken definition of prudence? Perhaps we have been led to this by witnessing

certain supposedly prudent people. As they have
exhibited the virtue it has not been very attractive.
We may have had painful experience of prudent
people. They never make a mistake, and they
never make anything else. Their only virtue
is that they never do anything rash or extraordinary. There is not a dash of heroism in
their nature. They are tame, monotonous. Yet
God says by Isaiah that Jesus Christ when He
comes shall be prudent. Surely prudence must
be a nobler quality than the supposedly prudent
suggest. Perchance we may have a fresh appreciation of true prudence as we see the beautifulness
of this element in the life of our Lord.

Really the prediction before us is grander than
it seems to be. The word rendered prudent
is a two-sided word, and, strangely enough, both
the Authorized and Revised Versions only bring
out one side of the significant word. Our
scholars say that the ideas of prudence and
prosperity are in the term. Bishop Chadwick
translates it " shall deal prudently, so that prosperity shall be the result." Very often prudence
fails, but the prudence of Christ is to succeed.
That is the idea of the text. By prudent methods
Christ is to achieve rule. By sagacity He is to
triumph. By insight He is to become a conqueror.

By far-seeing courses He shall scale the proudest throne of the universe. " Behold, My servant shall deal prudently." Let us think about the victorious prudence of Christ. An unfamiliar aspect of our Lord! It is almost foreign even to New Testament Christology. One man, however, realized it. Paul spoke of this divine prudence. In that marvellous first chapter of the marvellous Epistle to the Ephesians he dilates on "the riches of His grace which He hath made to abound in all wisdom, *and prudence*." Paul thinks of Christ's life as an exhibition of Godlike prudence.

Consider how this prophecy was fulfilled abundantly in the wisdom, carefulness, discretion of our incarnate Lord. See how prudently He dealt.

I. CHRIST DEALT PRUDENTLY IN NOT PRE-MATURELY SURRENDERING HIS LIFE.

He deemed His physical life a good gift of God, not to be parted with till His "hour" was assuredly come. His body He called a "temple," and He would not allow it to be sacrilegiously treated. He shunned premature death. Was He not prudent in this? We have several striking examples of His prudence. St. Luke tells us,

"They led Him to the brow of the hill whereon
their city was built, that they might cast Him
down headlong." He had aroused fierce wrath
as He preached at Nazareth, and the Nazarenes
sought thus to hurl Him to destruction. Did
He submit? No. The record of St. Luke is,
"But He passing through the midst of them
went His way." He dealt prudently.

St. John affords us several illustrations of this
particular form of prudence. His amazing word
spoken in the temple, "Before Abraham was I
am," so aroused the anger of the listeners that
"they took up stones to cast at Him." Did He
submit to their stoning? No. "Jesus hid Himself."
The suggestive reading of the R.V. margin is,
"Jesus was hidden." Almighty power manifested
itself and environed Him. "Jesus hid Himself
and went out of the temple." He dealt prudently.

After another of his most heart-searching
utterances we read that Jesus "hid Himself."
After the resurrection of Lazarus, "Jesus walked
no more openly among the Jews." On yet
another occasion, when it seemed as if His enemies
had secured Him, we read that "He went forthwith out of their hand."

It was most notable prudence. Till He knew
His work was done He would not allow His

life to be squandered. He came to earth to die, but He refused to die prematurely.

What an example for every Christlike servant of the world! Such should, like the Saviour, deal prudently. Prize your life, not excessively but moderately. Guard the temple of your body. Do not let it be destroyed before the divinely-appointed time. I need not urge this, for to plead with most modern Christians to take care of themselves would be too palpable an irony. But let him who needs the word receive it. Do not prematurely wear yourself down or be worn down. Work prudently. Do more by sometimes doing less. Such prudence is essential to ultimate and permanent success.

II. CHRIST'S PRUDENCE APPEARS IN HIS INSIGHT INTO CHARACTER.

" Behold, My servant shall deal prudently." In nothing did He fulfil this prophecy more markedly than in His deportment towards varying types of character. What insight the man Christ Jesus showed! Look at His New Testament biography, and see how wonderfully He discerned people. He read those who to others were a sealed book. Sealed scrolls were to Him unfolded scrolls. He saw right down into the soul. He could certainly

divine.   People He met for the first time He knew
at once.   Deep is that comment of St. John, " He
needed not that any should testify of man, for
He knew what was in man."   How the instances
of Christ's insight into character multiply upon us !
It is penetration which explains His bearing toward
men.   The rich young ruler is almost an idyllic
case.   Jesus beholding him (I suppose for the
first time) " loved him."   He saw into the depths
of that young heart.   He knew that, despite all
his crude conceptions of theology, and his equally
crude conceptions of the moral law, there were
lovely qualities in him.   His soul was a beautiful
garden.   And He " loved " him.   He dealt prudently towards that young ruler.   Christ's insight
never failed and was perfect in its fulness.   Of the
ecclesiastics of His age we are told that Jesus
" perceived their craftiness."   Beneath the elaborate
robes of sanctity He discovered the crafty heart
which has so often appertained to ecclesiastics.
There were Jesuits before there was Roman
Catholicism.   These men were Jesuits, they looked
innocent, as guilty people often do.   They seemed
in their assumed blamelessness, superbly unconscious of any evil.   But Jesus read their crooked
hearts.   He dealt prudently towards them.

It is our Lord's matchless insight which is the

secret of His apparently incongruous attitude to
certain people. Nicodemus approached Him in
gushing manner and offered Him an unsolicited
testimonial. "Master, we know that Thou art a
teacher come from God, for no man can do these
miracles that Thou doest, except God be with him."
Had Nicodemus come to us with such compliments
he would have taken us by storm. But Jesus
knew the heart of the man and with sovereign
insight He abruptly said, "Except a man be born
again he cannot see the kingdom of God." As if
to say, " The great concern is not what *I* am, but
what *you must become.*" Christ dealt prudently, and
insisted on the rectification of human character,
not the eulogy of divine quality. How prudently
He dealt with Pilate. Pilate was a dramatist and
varied his tone with rare power. Now he spoke
hectoringly and now sympathetically, but he
evoked no response from Jesus. He answered him
not a word. That non-answer was the best answer.
Christ knew that no word of His would reach
that heart. Silence was supremest prudence.

Still does He deal prudently. For this prophecy
is an eternal prophecy. And still in this especial
sense He is prudent. He knows us and acts
towards us with unerring wisdom. It is Christ's
perception of us which explains Christ's treatment

of us. He knows what we need at His hands.
His ways towards us are grounded upon divinest
insight. If He seem to deal hardly with us it is
because He knows our immediate need better far
than we can know it. I cannot understand why
He permits certain experiences which are mine.
But I will rest on this truth, that He best knows
what I need. His dealings are the outcome of
His knowledge of my heart. If I cannot always
say, "Thy will be done," He will wait patiently
till through grace I can say it. If I strive to
say it and fail, He will credit me with the devout
desire. Blessed for ever be the prudent Saviour!

III. The Adroitness of His Replies is a
Great Evidence of His Prudence.

Christ was always receiving deputations, now
friendly and now inimical. How wonderfully He
invariably dealt with them! Rapier-like in their
keen thrusts were His answers. Inimitable was
He in this as in all things. When He was but
twelve years old the people in the temple were
"amazed at His answers." And ever afterwards
His answers amazed all men. "The childhood
showed the man as morning shows the day." What
a course of sermons might be preached on the
answers of Jesus! Oh His prudent dealing! St.

Luke tells us of a deputation which approached Him and the historian prepares us for underhand work, for he tells us the men were "spies." They came to Christ with this problem, "Is it lawful to give tribute to Cæsar?" That was a very subtle question. Had He not been supremely prudent they would have trapped Him. Suppose He had replied, "No, it is not lawful"; they would have proclaimed Him a traitor to the Empire. But had He said, "Yes, it is lawful," they would have denounced Him as a truckler to the Roman Emperor. What did He reply? Did they catch Him? No. He caught them. "Show me a penny," is His demand; and bringing Him the coin He asks, "Whose image and superscription hath it?" And He replies, "Render unto Cæsar the things that are Cæsar's, and unto God the things that are God's." Oh the infinite prudence of that reply! A man who could so retort has a prudence which evokes our completest confidence. Take another example. A deputation came to Him asking by what "authority" He did the revolutionary and amazing things He wrought. What was His response? "The baptism of John, was it from heaven, or of men?" The humour and divine subtlety of that inquiry in that connection! They are hoist on their own petard. They reason, " If we say, From heaven, He will say, Why do ye not, then, believe on him ? But if we say, Of men, they feared the people, for all held John to be a prophet. And they said, We cannot tell. Jesus answered, Neither tell I you by what authority I do these things." Did He not deal prudently ? Look at one further instance. A case of a very different kind presented itself. The Sadducees brought a strange incident to His notice. I think probably it was an apocryphal story—that of the woman who had seven husbands. Poor woman ! " In the resurrection whose wife shall she be ? " Mark the cunning of that inquiry. Had our Lord not been dowered with wondrous prudence how He might have been snared by such an adroit eschatological question. How sublime His answer, " In the resurrection they neither marry nor are given in marriage, but are as the angels of God " ! A ray of welcome light on the eternal world ! A proof of divinest prudence ! Not surprised are we to read of one of the scribes that he knew " He had answered them well." Nor are we astonished that it is written, " Neither durst any man ask Him any question." Most assuredly, in His adroitness of reply, God's Servant, dealt prudently.

He still deals prudently herein. We can take

our present problems to the Divine man ascended. How wonderful are His answers still! He is evermore "this same Jesus." His reply to your appeals may not have been such as you desired, but it has been appropriate to you. Christ's answers have appropriateness to the man who is being answered. Our Lord knows you through and through. He looks upon the question in the light of the questioner. Take all your hard questions to the greater than Solomon. He may delay to answer. But the very delay is education. Ultimately He will give the answer that shall be rest unto your soul. "My soul, wait thou only upon" the still-incarnate God!

IV. CHRIST'S PRUDENCE IS SEEN IN HIS CONCESSIONS TO THE LIMITATIONS OF HIS HEARERS.

As a preacher or teacher He dealt prudently, and here is one arrestive manifestation of this. I want you to admire not only His knowledge, and eloquence, and sympathy, but His prudence. Many a public teacher is destroyed through lack of prudence. Christ was established by His prudence. How prudently He dealt in uttering a specially difficult truth! "He that is able to receive it, let him receive it," is His wise word.

Everybody is not called upon to receive every hard or mysterious truth. Suppose a reverent, earnest soul is not able to accept a particular doctrine, then the Lord does not urge it upon him. Christ will never put a cross upon the intellect that the intellect is unable to bear. Still, Christ only asks men to receive for the time being truths they are able to receive. O prudent Teacher divine!

How prudently He dealt in graduating truth. He spake (says Mark) "as they were able to hear it." He adapted what He said to the people to whom he said it. I fear some of us preach certain sermons to our congregations whether or no they are able to hear them. We forget Christ's great law of prudent adaptation. We give theology where there is only capacity for anecdotes. We address children as if they were philosophers or scientists. "As they were able to hear it." Magnificent secret of truly successful preaching and teaching!

He graduated truth not only in respect of its quality but its season. "I have yet many things to say unto you, but ye cannot bear them now," is an utterance which John has preserved for us. The unseasonable truth is for you an impotent truth. The things that could not then be borne by His followers He has since spoken from heaven through His inspired Apostles. The apostolic epistles are the higher developments of our Lord's teaching.

Let us as preachers and Christian teachers by Christ's grace emulate His prudence. Be adaptive. Consider your hearers. Modulate your tone according to the ear to which you speak. The all-prudent Saviour still makes His old concessions to our limitations. He hath compassion on our weakness. He varies His manner of teaching. He goes softly for our sakes. He speaks now in parable, now by concrete symbol, now in proverb, and now in deep oracle. O ever-prudent Christ! "Speak, Lord, for Thy servant heareth."

V. BY HIS ENCOURAGEMENT OF GOOD CHRIST DEALT PRUDENTLY.

Who saw latent good in everyone as He did! Who praised nascent excellence like Him! He delighted to accredit a soul. He joyed with high joy in all discoveries of truth and purity. He told the scribe he was "not far from the kingdom of God." He commended the religionists of the day in this: "Ye search the Scriptures." He shed the light of hope on a penitent woman by saying, "Neither do I condemn thee." This was His encomium upon a pardoned one, "She loved much." Said He to His sorrowing disciples, "Already ye are clean."

Was not this lovely prudence? Is it not always highest prudence to encourage all good, however incipient, in all souls? Do you strive after such prudence? Cheer thyself, O honest earnest soul! The Lord credits the good that is in thee. "A bruised reed shall He not break, and the smoking flax shall He not quench." Trust His infinite magnanimity if thou art found in the way of righteousness.

VI. Christ's Prudence was the Larger Prudence.

The little timid prudence, the peddling prudence, was not our Lord's type of prudence. There is the prudence of a mouse and there is the prudence of a lion. Christ's was leonine prudence. His was not the prudence of many so-called prudent people, which is but the instinct of self-preservation acutely developed. Christ's was the noble, the sacrificial prudence. Splendid self-sacrifice is the highest prudence. "Behold, My servant shall deal prudently" is really the text of that wondrous redemption-chapter, the fifty-third of Isaiah. "He was led as a lamb to the

slaughter." Was that prudent? "He bare the
sin of many." Was that prudent? It was heroic,
it was redeeming, but was it prudence? God
says it was. And indeed it was. It is the larger
prudence. Estimate prudence by the Eternal.
Take long views of prudence. "He that loseth
his life shall find it." To be sacrificial is to deal
prudently. Christ's grandest prudence was exhibited on Calvary. Redemption is divinest
prudence. Be ours, in our poor remote degree,
this self-renouncing prudence.

VII. CHRIST DEALT PRUDENTLY IN HIS
PROCURAL OF SALVATION.

What the old evangelicals termed "the plan of
salvation" represents transcendent prudence. Its
method is prudent in degree. O the far-sightedness
of such a method! The Son of God took pity on
our flesh and blood. He took hold of it. He
became our brother. He atoned for us by His
death on the cross. Through death He won us
everlasting life. Most wonderful prevision marks
that method of redemption. There is equal prudence in the condition of salvation. Salvation by
faith, by trustfulness, by reliance! By such a
method God reaches *the many*. It is a condition

of which a little child is capable.   Whosoever will come may thus come.

Astonishing prudence shines in God's salvation. Let each of us penitently accept it.   Let us escape to Calvary lest we be consumed.   Say ye, "The Saviour died for me."   O God of glory, we humbly and gratefully receive the reconciliation wrought so prudently and so prudently offered to us !

> O loving wisdom of our God !
>   When all was sin and shame,
> A second Adam to the fight
>   And to the rescue came.
>
> O *wisest* love that flesh and blood
>   That did in Adam fail,
> Should strive again against the foe,
>   Should strive and should prevail !

XI

WISDOM FAILS. FOOLISHNESS SUCCEEDS

" For after that in the wisdom of God the world by wisdom knew not God, it pleased God by the foolishness of preaching to save them that believe."—I COR. i. 21.

ONE of our great works of biblical learning characterizes my text as " this difficult verse," and unquestionably it is difficult. But the intricate passages of Scripture are often the noblest. Those portions of the word of God which involve mental concentration well repay assiduous study. It is worth breaking a hard shell if it contain a sweet kernel. It is not lost labour to delve for fine gold. An iron casket which demands patience and skill to open is eminently recompensive if rare gems burn within. So let us wholeheartedly address ourselves to " this difficult verse." When we remember what the learned and saintly Godet says, we are expectant, for he declares, " The verse contains in three lines a whole philo-

sophy of history, the substance of entire volumes."
We are called to ponder a dark fact of history
and a bright fact of history.

I. WE ARE BROUGHT FACE TO FACE WITH A DARK FACT OF HISTORY.

"In the wisdom of God the world by wisdom
knew not God." The verse opens with a logical
term, evidently, therefore, we have to do with an
argument. This verse is the proof of the preceding
verse. Paul there almost ridiculingly asks, "Where
is the wise? Where is the scribe? Where is the
disputer of this world?" Then comes the crucial
question, the great idea he strives to demonstrate,
"Hath not God made foolish the wisdom of this
world?" This is a rhetorical inquiry. Paul in
interrogatory form asserts that God *has* made
foolish the wisdom of this world. If we ask for
his evidence he is ready with it, it is found in our
text; that explains the "for" which heads the
verse. Tell us, open-eyed, logical Paul, what proof
there is that God has confounded human learning
in saving humanity. Show us how, if it be indeed
so, God has reduced "wise" and "scribe" and "disputer" to the vanishing point. Hear the *factual*
testimony! "*For*, seeing that in the wisdom of
God the world through its wisdom knew not God,

it was God's good pleasure through the foolishness of the preaching to save them that believe" (R.V.).

The general argument indicated by that inaugural " for " is that God has made human learning, as a means of knowing God, ridiculous by reason of its *impotence* in the spiritual world. And this in two respects. (*a*) Learning did not give the knowledge of God. (*β*) What seemed foolishness imparted that knowledge. We can never overlook the evidential value of those great historical facts. Now to their examination.

I call this a dark fact of history. Is it not? " In the wisdom of God the world by wisdom knew not God." If you accept that statement then it is positively history's darkest fact.

But is it true? We shall do well to discuss the terms of the statement with some minuteness.

What is the meaning of the phrase " in the wisdom of God "? Define the force of that " in."

I have frequently heard it set forth as if it meant *as a result of*. So interpreted the phrase would mean that it was the determination of God's wisdom that the world by wisdom should not know God. In other words, just as we speak of a man or a body of men doing thus and so in his or their wisdom, so Paul asseverates here that it was the result of God's wise purpose that the world by its wisdom knew not God. That is a very usual exposition. Now I cannot for a moment accept that exposition. See what such an interpretation involves. It means that it was the decree of God that human wisdom should fail to know God. It means that this was the decision of Divine Wisdom. I cannot conceive of God ordaining that serious earnest wisdom should utterly fail in its attempts to know Him. I cannot conceive of God fore-dooming any honest method of seeking Him. Especially I cannot imagine that it was God's set purpose to brand the mind of man with infamy. No. I believe Dr. Beet has given us the true view of the phrase. " In " here carries its most natural meaning. You speak of a man being in the air, in the earth, in the sea : in the same sense Paul uses the tiny but significant word. Dr. Beet renders it " amid." " Amid the wisdom of God the world through the wisdom (that wisdom) knew not God." The world was " in," amid, the wisdom of God, it was encompassed by it, and yet it failed to know God by that wisdom. Verily that is indeed and of a truth a dark historical fact. But we must analyse the fact into its parts that we may test it fully. Are any links of the chain weak ?

Paul says the world was "*in* the wisdom of God." In it like an atmosphere. In it like a sphere. In it like a crystal ocean. A wonderful thought! From the earliest days the world was environed by the wisdom of God. By the world he means humanity as a whole. This is obviously true. There is no need to argue such a fact. It is axiomatic. But it is well worth examining.

Around man has ever swept in imposing grandeur the circle of God's wisdom : let us note a segment or so of that radiant circle.

(*a*) Humanity has continually been amid the wisdom of God *in Nature*. Creation is an expression of God's wisdom. It is embodied wisdom. "The meanest flower that blows" is eloquent of God's wisdom. You need never lack an interesting and instructive sermon if you have a flower in your room. The smallest star that twinkles in the vault of heaven utters a splendid proclamation concerning the wisdom of God. From the beginning God's wisdom has been shown in Nature. Modern science has greatly enhanced the view of that wisdom. The Bible teaches that Nature has a moral and spiritual value : that Creation is a revelation of God, and that man is responsible for the apologetic element in it. The Bible does not hesitate to claim that humanity cannot be held innocent if it ignore the God who is concealed and yet revealed in Nature. So far my text is correct. Nature which so surrounds him makes man to be " in the wisdom of God."

(*b*) Humanity is "in the wisdom of God" *in social life*. No thoughtful mind can contemplate social life without seeing in it a manifestation of divine wisdom. Man has been social from the beginning. Society with its varied intelligences and its influences is a revelation of God's wisdom.

(*c*) *History* makes man to be " in the wisdom of God." We speak of the hand of God in history, and well we may. If history is not to man a continuous display of divine wisdom, man must indeed be crass. Is it not the deepest philosophy of history that it is divine wisdom? I can find no clue to the maze of history but this, that divine wisdom is operant there. A volume of history is a work on the evidences.

(*d*) Then, part of the " world" of which Paul speaks was "in the wisdom of God" in another sense: they had *the Scriptures*. The Jews (he alludes to them as a section of " the world" in ver. 22) had the Old Testament. There we read God's name in fairer lines. What a revelation is the Bible of the wisdom of God! Who can read its mystic pages without worshipping God as " the only wise God " ? Christ declared that the Old Testament was sufficient to make any man repent. The Bible-reading world was ever in the wisdom of God.

It is, then, a fact of history, as Paul asserts, that humanity is " in (amid) the wisdom of God." History repeats itself. Surely *this* history does. The world of to-day is peculiarly "in the wisdom of God." You are, my friends, in a far fuller and more responsible degree than were the peoples of the past. The wisdom of God is your environment. It compasses you about. You are *in* it, and cannot get away from it.   Nature, Society, History, Scripture—these ministrants are at your service as never before. Take heed lest you are oblivious of God's wisdom. It cannot do everything for you, but it can do much. It cannot save you, but it can contribute to your salvation.

Now we turn to the second part of this fact which makes it so dark. Paul says, "the world by wisdom knew not God." This seems contradictory of his teaching in the first chapter of his Epistle to the Romans, where he urges that men know God through Nature, and so are " without excuse." There is really no iota of contradiction when you recollect the sense the word "know" bears. You must interpret "knew not God" in the light of the latter part of the verse. It is equivalent to "save." Paul here speaks of *saving* knowledge of God. In a sense the world knew God, *e.g.*, they knew His existence and His power, but they knew not His redeeming love. And, as it has been well put, "Not to know that God loves us is not to know God."

The world by the manifold wisdom of God amid which it dwelt did not acquire a saving knowledge of God. That is Paul's bold declaration. God's all-surrounding wisdom did not prove the medium of the knowledge of God. "The world"—Greeks, Jews, Romans—particularly the cultured world, "knew not God."

You have not so read history as to be prepared to deny that fact. You know it to be a fact. Dr. Marcus Dods says of this Pauline statement, "No safer assertion regarding the ancient world can be made." Did Socrates, Plato, Aristotle, the very flower of the ancient world, know God in the warm, vivid, blessed sense? Assuredly this is a dark fact of history. "Amid the wisdom of God the world by wisdom knew not God."

How powerless is the intellect to give us the fullest knowledge of God! As Matthew Henry quaintly has it, " The heathen politicians and philosophers, the Jewish rabbis and doctors, the curious searchers into the secrets of Nature, were all posed and put to a nonplus. " The world by wisdom knew not God."

History repeats itself. Yes indeed! I challenge you to disprove this as a present-day fact. Does the world by wisdom know God now ? Assuredly not with *saving* knowledge of which Paul spoke. The world cultured, fashionable, rich, ecclesiastical, moral, does not know God. They know Him to be, but not to be what He is—atoning love. Perchance certain of you know not God. You are always amid His wisdom, but do you know Him ? How foolish is the wisdom of this world ! Why not seek the deeper, fuller, saving knowledge now ? Do not be content to be " an infant crying in the night." " God is light," and, through redeeming grace, you may " walk in the light."

II. What a sweet relief to turn now to A BRIGHT FACT OF HISTORY !

Nay! It is of all historic facts the brightest. And this shining truth springs out of a recognition of the sombre reality we have just faced.

God has " made foolish the wisdom of this world." Paul says, in effect, He was compelled to make it foolish. Why? "Seeing that amid the wisdom of God the world by wisdom knew not God." Now comes this bright and blessed truth. "It was God's good pleasure." R.V. ("Because it was good in fact."—Godet). What a hint of divine grace! What a suggestion that it was God's *kindness* which devised the way of salvation! "It was God's good pleasure through the foolishness of the preaching to save them that believe." What does that mean? It is a much misunderstood sentence. It is supposed to mean that God saves through preaching, and that preaching is a foolish instrumentality. That is not at all the meaning. Is preaching a foolish thing? I do not deny that some of it has been very foolish. But the art or instrumentality is in itself anything but foolish. From the earliest time God has used the ordinance of preaching. Would He be likely to call into service an intrinsically foolish force? By no means. Moreover preaching is an instrumentality which is utilized in other spheres as well as in religion. The equivalent of preaching is found at work everywhere and always has been. So there is nothing essentially foolish about preaching. But some say that "the foolishness of preaching" refers to the fact that the people thought preaching to be foolish.

Unhappily for such an exposition this is not a fact. The art of preaching has never been deemed foolish except by persons themselves incapable of it. Poor feeble preaching has always been thought to be foolish, and such it is. But never has adequate preaching been disesteemed. Such preaching has always been popular. It is the most popular force of the Churches to-day. Was Paul's preaching thought to be foolish? In no wise. They rejected his message perchance, but they owned the impressiveness of the forms in which the message was clothed. Even those who mocked Paul's gospel loved to hear him preach. Assuredly preaching was not reckoned foolishness.

It is in quite another direction we must look for the meaning of " the foolishness of preaching." You will find in the margin of the R.V. that the literal rendering is "the foolishness of the thing preached." Now we have the true idea. " It was God's good pleasure through the foolishness of the thing preached to save them that believe." Because the world failed to know God savingly by wisdom He decided to save it by foolishness. It is the *subject* of Christian preaching that men have deemed foolishness. Paul is speaking quotatively. The cultured Greeks sneered at the preaching of Christ crucified as "foolishness." "We preach Christ crucified—unto the Greeks foolishness" (ver. 23). Paul, that master of retort, finely replies that it is "the foolishness of God," and that such "foolishness" is "wiser than men."

A glorious verity this! It is God's good pleasure to save believers by the preaching of this divine "foolishness," a crucified Christ. It was this that was *the* theme of apostolic preaching. Of many other matters those early preachers spake, but this was their central and fundamental theme. So it must be to-day if men are to be saved.

Christ crucified is the mystery of mysteries, but we are not saved by comprehension but by faith. In this as in all religious truth I must believe where I cannot prove.

I preach this sublime and pathetic foolishness as the one ground of salvation. When I accept it with a reliant mind and heart and will, I have cleansing from all my guilt, and I receive God's Spirit into my heart to enable me to overcome the power of sin and achieve God's holy will.

Still the world reckons this preaching "foolishness." And even in the modern Church there seem to be many "Greeks" who entertain a similar opinion. The silence on this supreme theme in numerous pulpits is ominous. If this is the only gospel of salvation, how appalling is the silence! Is the "foolishness" generally, clearly, and un-equivocally preached? They are worthy of sore impeachment who are so criminally silent. Is there any other way of salvation? Assuredly no. The New Testament knows of no salvation by our Lord's lovely character. It speaks not of salvation by His peerless earthly life. Nor does it publish salvation by means of Christ's ideal teachings. It is Christ the Gospel, not Christ the Gospeller, of which God's Word makes such insistent mention. According to the Saviour and His apostles, it is the death divine that saves men, and that alone. The apostles say far more of the death than of any other element of the Lord's earthly history. Many to-day shift the centre of gravity from Christ's death to His life. If this be right the New Testament is flagrantly wrong. It suffices for many of us that such teaching is unscriptural. We stand or fall by the Scriptures. To those who reject the apostolic teaching as fallible we have no word. To us that teaching is infallible. We accept it as final. Oh, hold ye to the sure word! What "wisdom" never does this "foolishness" always does—it saves

them that believe.   The key of the eternal situation is in the preaching of the divine " foolishness."

Do we not well to remind ourselves of the close
association between the " foolishness " and " the
preaching " ?   Preaching is the God-decreed agency
for making known the crucified Saviour.   Preaching
as an ordinance is part of " God's good pleasure."
There has been no revocation of this supreme
ordinance.   By this weapon evangelical Churches
have ever conquered in the fight.   Nothing gathers
the multitude and converts the multitude as evangelical preaching does.   Preaching is not merely
as between man and man, but it is between God
and man.   It is *the* sacrament.   Of all acts of
worship it is the most helpful.   The Churches
grieve God's Spirit when they ignore or depreciate
preaching.   May not this explain the barrenness
of many Churches ?   Let no miscalled " priest "
push his " altar " to the front.   The pulpit, not the
altar, is the Christian symbol.   Nor let any
" organisation " overshadow the ministry of preaching.   This is a crying peril in Protestant as well as
Roman Catholic Churches.   We must keep the
preacher to the front. We must enforce the
divinely-appointed channel of the divinely-ordained
" foolishness."

God's purpose is to " save " by the holy foolishness. The moment faith is reposed in the crucified Christ the guilt of a man's past is pardoned and he is accepted of God. Oh, is not this good news? This is the gospel indeed. "Believest *thou* this?" Oh, know ye assuredly that no deeds of thine can effect this wondrous issue, nor can any merit of thine, however cherished. There is no forgiveness, no justification of God, except by simple faith in Christ's atoning sacrifice. Thus and only thus God "saves."

But there is a further meaning in this great word "save." It has an ethical signification. It refers to the attainment of character, the adorning with spiritual beauty, the riddance of sin from the heart, and the inspiring of the nature with power to live a Jesus-like life. It is faith in a crucified Saviour which evokes this ethical salvation. The atonement of Christ is the fount of purity. Character-building begins at the foot of the cross. Let history and experience speak and they will testify that faith in the crucified has created the finest character. The noblest morality is reared at Calvary. All the loveliest flowers bloom on that rugged height. A reliant faith in the dying Saviour changes the nature. Are we ethically saved? Does our evangelicalism attest its potency in our daily life? We must emphasize this aspect of salvation. Recognize no salvation that is not proved by a beautiful life. The morality of the crucified is as matchless as His theology is profound. The cross changes the life as well as the sentiments and the emotions. My increasing hope for the morality of the world lies in "the foolishness of preaching." The quality of the salvation it effects is the warrant of the gospel.

What is the instrumental cause of this great salvation? It is believing God saves "them that believe" in the crucified Christ. There is sad danger of a shallow use of that word "believe." To believe, in the scriptural sense, involves the consent of the heart by trustfulness, of the mind by apprehension, of the will by subjugation. None "believe" who are not thus affected in those three centres of their being. Are you of "them that believe"? What is your attitude towards "the foolishness"? May the atoning death of our Lord secure the assent of your intellect, the devotion of your heart, and the surrender of your will!

Surely it is the brightest of historic facts that God has devised such a method of salvation. Sound out everywhere the silver trumpet of the gospel! Oh that we all may be enrolled among the happy host of "them that believe."

What a cluster of antitheses is here! Wisdom

fails, and—as if it might be, as one suggests, the punishment of reason for its sin—foolishness succeeds.   Men "knew not God"—and God saves. "The world" is out in the cold, and "them that believe" are introduced into light and warmth. By wisdom, none realized God aright ; by believing, men have saving realisation.

Let these great evangelical truths sway and mould our life and thought. Be it ours, by believing "the foolishness of preaching," to be saved with a great and everlasting salvation. God speed this mighty gospel !

XII

THE EVER-EVIDENT CHRIST

"He could not be hid."—MARK vii. 24.

IT was a fact. It is a truth. And the ageless truth is even more remarkable than the historical fact. Let those who note the striking fact adore the glorious truth.

I. CHRIST'S PERSONALITY PREVENTS HIS BEING HID.

So it was when He "went into the borders of Tyre and Sidon," and so it for ever is. "He entered into an house," but the people of that heathen region had heard of Him who He was. Hence, though "He would have no man know" of His presence, "He could not be hid." Such personality will out. As Matthew Henry has it, "A candle may be put under a bushel, the sun cannot." The solar presence of the Lord irradiated every region in which it tarried.

Personality is the greatest and grandest thing in the universe. Potent personality cannot be inconspicuous. You may eclipse it awhile, but you cannot extinguish it. Great personality is always " the chariots of Israel and the horsemen thereof." Jesus Christ in personality as in all things has the pre-eminence. Verily He cannot be hid.

" Thou seemest human and divine," we reverently cry as we behold Him travelling in the greatness of His strength along the pathway of the ages. And it is the unheard-of blending of the human and divine that makes His personality so unique and wonderful.

How could or can such a personality be hid ? He was evidently man, but He was all but as evidently God. The implication of the birth in Bethlehem was a pre-existence in heaven. There were not wanting signs that the babe in the manger was " Father of eternity." What a strange association there was in His infancy of earthly lowliness and celestial glory ! And that same unprecedented combination followed Him all the days of His redeeming sojourn here. Oh the mystery of that personality ! How could He be hid ? Could He ever have been meant to be hid ?

They who knew Him best were most deeply persuaded of His being divine as well as human. He received deepest and most worshipful recognition from them who had companied with Him all the time. He was more than " Rabbi " to those who were in the secret of His presence. He was " the Christ " and " Lord " and " God."

O marvellous personality ! A poor man, yet carrying Himself and declaring Himself as one who had a divine history behind Him and divine resources at His instant disposal. Sitting weary on Jacob's well, yet offering rest to all labouring and heavy-laden souls. Poorer than the poorest, yet claiming to make men richer than the richest. Homeless, and yet speaking of heaven as " where He was before " ; yea, declaring Himself to be " in heaven " even whilst treading the inhospitable earth. Avowing that He died of His own free will. He could coerce the last enemy. He could laugh the grave to scorn. He proclaimed Himself older than Abraham. He declared Himself invested with " all authority." Was there ever His like ? *Ecc Homo! Ecce Deus !* " He could not be hid."

On the moral side His personality is distinctly human and divine. He searches and expounds the Scriptures. He prays without ceasing. In

everything He gives thanks.   He worships in the
temple.   He is man.   He is our fellow-believer.
But He cries, "Which of you convinceth Me of
sin ? "   The holiest saint never dared or dreamed
to speak thus.   The whitest souls shrink with
most acute sensitiveness from such a challenge.
The meek and lowly Jesus uttered the challenge !
He was sinless, and knew Himself to be such,
and proclaimed Himself to be such.   Explain it.
Annotate adequately so unknown a circumstance.
I assert without reserve that His sinlessness is
the supreme evidence of His Deity.   To be such
a man He must have been God.

He was a Saviour too.   He saved men from
sickness, and sorrow, and death.   But He did far
more.   He was a Saviour from sin—that tap-root
of sickness, and sorrow, and death.   He delivered
men from base habits.   He transfigured character.
He turned the human and the diabolic to
divine.

Do you marvel that " He could not be hid " ?
Supreme conspicuousness must be the lot of
such an one.   There is only one sun, though there
be many stars and satellites.   Shall the Sun of
righteousness be hid ?   Surely not.   Being what
He was " He could not be hid."   A lesser personality might be shrouded in obscurity, but the glory

of such an orb of day must attest itself everywhere.

This is an *eternal* circumstance. Jesus Christ never has been and never can be absolutely hid. Jesus may have been hid, but Jesus' *Christ* never. In Old Testament times my text was a fact. My text was true centuries upon centuries before it was written. Facts are facts recorded or unrecorded. The Saviour was the Saviour or ever He was historified.

Before His incarnation He could not be hid. His glory flashed upon Eden when the protevangelism was proclaimed. He tarried among the patriarchs; and was not hid from their believing eyes. He was with Israel in the wilderness and in Canaan, nor did faithful eyes fail to discern Him. No, He was not hid from prophets and kings and priests and psalmists and lowly souls in the dispensation of imperfect times.

Is He hid to you as you read your Old Testament? Are your eyes opened as you peruse the wonderful records? Seest thou One like unto the Son of man? Except He be the very life of the Old Testament to you it will indeed be an *Old* Testament and will be ready to vanish away. To illumined eyes in no cranny of the Old Testament can Christ be hid.

As in Old Testament times and as in New Testament times, so now, in these times, Jesus Christ cannot be hid. Men of low design have striven hard to hide Him. If He could have been hid He would have been by now. Hell has been moved to hide Him, but it has disquieted itself in vain. Was it ever so manifest as now that our Lord cannot be hid?

Not to speak of all the preaching, and all the praying, and all the literature of apologetics and of devotion—what a wonderful interest there is in Jesus Christ! The press is ever discussing Him, either as to His person, or His principles, or His achievements. Let a novel appear which deals with any aspect of Christology, and what popular interest it evokes. Novelists essay to write the life of Christ. The masses are deeply and ineradically interested in Jesus. Quite as true is it outside the Churches as within them that He cannot be hid. He is more famous after nineteen centuries than before. To the chagrin of his foes He *cannot* be hid. It is the hell of hell, and it is the heaven of heaven. Nor while earth remains can He be hid. Thrones will rock and perish, but His shall neither rock nor perish. All and in all Jesus is, and shall be. Here is the Christ's future history as well as His

past history—" He could not be hid." My text
is prophecy, and not history alone. He continueth
ever and the same for ever, therefore shall He not
for evermore be hid. Nor must we limit this eternal
fact to earth. In heaven Christ cannot be hid.
He never was hidden there. All the angels of
God worshipped Him. He was not hid from
the heavenly hosts whilst He was incarnate here.
" The mystery of godliness " was " seen of
angels," and they evinced their reverential interest
in Him. He is this moment and all the golden
moments of heaven adored above all adoration
by the hosts in glory. This is the history of
heaven, its highest history—" He could not be
hid."

You know why, when He entered " the borders
of Tyre and Sidon," He could not be hid?
" He would have no man know it"; that was
His desire, though not His decree, and despite
His desire, " He could not be hid." You know
why? It was His unspeakable personality. Yes.
But what caused His personality to be known
in that heathen tract of country? His followers
had spread His fame abroad. Many of them
had come to Tyre and Sidon after Him. They
could not rest away from Him. Is that so with
you? Do you take care that He shall not be

hid? Oh, spread His fame abroad! Tell it, be always telling it, to your children, to your household, to the world. Go ye to Tyre and Sidon as His followers and heralds and apostles. Whether men will hear or forbear, publish the name that is above every name. Do your uttermost that from no man shall He be hid.

Is He hid from you? Do you see Jesus who He is? Be Simeon's song yours, in youth and in age, " Mine eyes have seen Thy salvation."

II. SOME THINGS IN CHRIST ARE HID.

Being man we can perceive much of His personality, but being God-man we realize that there is in Him much we cannot discern. He hints to us not only God's knowableness, but also God's unknowableness. As a whole He cannot be hid, but He can be and is partially hid. The riches of Christ are "not to be traced out." Into the " things " of the Saviour the angels cannot completely penetrate. All the revelations of God have and must have their mysterious elements, and such elements we find in Him who is the supreme revelation of God. That is a great deep word of Paul's in his Epistle to the Colossians, " In whom are hid all the treasures of wisdom and knowledge." The scholars tell

us there is special emphasis upon the term " hid."
We see many of those ineffable treasures in Him,
but how many that we know to be there are
"hid." Yet even these are not hid absolutely.
They are hid from us for the time being, but to
patient faith and holy meditation, and Christian
experience they reveal themselves. Christ becomes less and less " hid " to His followers as
they follow on to know Him. He discovers Himself to them. They see Him in His own light.

Are you often perplexed that so much of Christ
is hidden from you? Think it not strange. It is
the common lot of the saints. " The same afflictions are accomplished in your brethren that are
in the world." Can we expect the God-man to be
easily understood? Thank God, much of Him a
little child may know. Babes and sucklings are oft-
times prize-taking scholars in the Saviour's school.
But there are ethereal heights in Christ which
can only be attained by wings that have been
strengthened by successive flights. Be patient,
brethren! Our Lord is never absolutely hid from
you. He cannot be hid from seeing eyes. You
see Him much more vividly than once you did.
You shall see Him with ever-growing clarity of
vision till you on heaven's songful heights "see
Him as He is."

III. Sometimes Christ Seeks to be Hid.

There is a sense in which Christ can and will be hid. Language cannot be applied to Him in a stereotyped sense, so we say that, whilst from one point of view He cannot be hid, yet from another He determines at times to be hid. Alas! He is hid anon *because of our sins.* The older religious teachers laid great stress on this. They emphasized the admonitory fact that through evil omissions or positive transgressions our Beloved withdraws Himself. It is indeed true. This is part of His discipline of us. Divine withdrawments are divine corrections. As a Christian believer my sins can cause my Saviour to be hid from me. ,He does not reveal Himself to impenitent transgressors. Till I confess my sins He will be concealed from my vision.

Oh these sins of mine! I hate them for many a reason, but most because they have hid my Lord from mine eyes as in a dark and noxious cloud. Is He hid from you because of some transgression? Pray Him to come back and flash His gracious glory upon eyes cleansed by penitential tears. Forsake the sin and thou shalt see the Saviour. He wills to be hid from those who have grieved Him, but He longingly

awaits their penitence that He may disclose
Himself to them again. He at times seeks to
be hid that He may save and help. He did thus
to His disciples when He was here. So He did
on the lake. So He did to the Emmaus travellers.
And His aforetime method He still uses. Often
He hides Himself in *events*. Every great and
significant event, joyous or sorrowful, is a coming
of Christ. But, alas! many allow the event to pass
without recognizing Him. He hides Himself in
persons. The beggar at your gate may bring the
appealing Christ to you. Oh, see that you fail
not to perceive Him. Christ hides Himself in
influences. Many of the influences that come
upon us are visitations of the Lord. He hides
in these that He may help us the more abundantly,
that He may educate us into a greater ability
to recognize Him.

Wise may we be to understand how Christ hides
Himself for our chastening and for our instruction!

IV. THERE ARE THOSE WHO CAUSE CHRIST
TO BE HID.

"He could not be hid." Ah, but some have a
fatal genius for hiding Him. We have almost
performed the evil miracle of blotting out the
sun. They who do not preach Him are such.

The pulpit may extinguish the Saviour it was built to uplift. Preaching may be a depreciation of Jesus. It may obscure Him instead of pouring light upon Him. Oh, what an irony and what a wickedness is a Christless pulpit! Is there not a peril of the pulpit preaching everything but Christ? In sermons as in all things He must have the pre-eminence. To hide Christ from the people is to perpetrate the cruellest of wrongs. It is to keep back light from them that walk in darkness, and bread from souls that perish of hunger. Preacher! Preach Jesus the Christ: Jesus always: Jesus only.

They hide Christ who do not preach Him *evangelically*. We may preach Jesus without preaching Christ. What a chasm there is between the unitarian Jesus and the redeeming Christ! It is not enough to proclaim our Lord's consummate ethical beauty and perfectness, nor His incomparable teachings, nor His pathetic martyrdom. The Saviour of the gospels and of the epistles is much more than this or He would not be a Saviour. Neither character, teachings, nor martyrdom make a Saviour. He who thus and thus only preaches Christ makes Him to be hid from men's eyes. Only the evangelical Saviour is the great and legitimate theme of preaching.

Jesus the God manifested in the flesh. Jesus bearing our sins in His own body on the tree, a mystery of substitution. Jesus raised from the dead for our justification. Jesus throned in heaven as our Intercessor. These are *the* messages of the pulpit. He hides the Saviour who neglects or conceals these cardinal realities. Oh, preach ye the evangelical Christ, the Saviour of all men!

When Christ is not lived He is hid. They who obey Him reveal Him. The life that is full of goodness is a guide to Him. How possible it is, however, to profess to believe Him as our Saviour, and yet to refuse Him as our Lord. We must do the things He says. We must walk even as He walked. If our daily life be not a reminder of Christ to others, we are hiding Him. No sermon reveals Christ as does a Christian life. Christlike lives are expositions of Christianity. Does your life reveal the Lord or does it hide Him? The direst possibility of each of us is that our conduct may shut off the Saviour from the vision and thought and love of men.

We hide Christ if we do not confess Him. In these times we prize all too lightly the verbal confession of our Lord. With the mouth confession must be made. We are pledged to confess with our mouth that God hath raised Christ from the dead. I know that character is the noblest confession, but we must not forget the scriptural duty of the word of confession. Testimony greatly languishes in the Churches. A dumb devil seems to possess many of God's people. "I have not hid Thy righteousness within my heart," said the grateful psalmist. But dare we say it? Do we ever confess Christ among men? A word unaffectedly spoken by us might be as a breath of heaven upon our friends. Oh, speak it at all cost of nerve or heart or strength! Tell others of the Lord who is so much to you. If He be all in all to you, surely you will not hide Him from men by an ungrateful silence.

It is a criminality to hide such a Saviour. The sick-hearted world needs Him sorely. Beware of hiding Him. Conceal not His loving-kindness and His truth. Sound forth the word of the Lord.

V. THERE ARE HALLOWED SPHERES IN WHICH CHRIST CANNOT BE HID.

He cannot be hid in the word of God. He breathes and shines through and through the sacred writings. In a truly Christian Church He cannot be hid. He is the life of all things therein. His real presence is the *rationale* of every institution and ceremony. He is the object and aim of every effort made.

In a truly Christian life Christ cannot be hid. Words and actions and abstinences alike tell of Him. A saintly character forces Christ upon the world's reluctant gaze. He never will be hid as long as earth contains one who adorns His teachings in all things.

There are few scenes in which it is more impossible to hide Christ than a Christian home. He pervades that Paradise Regained. He ever walks amid the fair expanses of that garden. It was there that many of us first saw Him. We were bewitched with Him. We cried, " Thou hast ravished my heart." Till we see Him in heaven we shall never see Him more sweet and fair than we saw Him in our early home. Is He clearly seen in your home? Is your meekness, lovableness, patience, geniality, self-denial a showing forth of Christ to all who know you? Hide not that Blessed One in your home. Let His glory flame through every chamber.

In a Christian sick chamber Christ cannot be hid. When His people are in the furnace sevenfold heated the " form of the fourth " is seen to the astonishment and delight of beholders. Where has the Lord been more gloriously displayed than in the sick room? There we have all seen Him pathetically displayed. When any suffers as a Christian he reveals the Lord's Christ.

In the death of a saint Christ cannot be hid. The life of the Lord triumphs in the death of a believer. The Saviour is pledged to be very near His people in their final hour. Nor does He ever break His pledge. Many have become His disciples because they have seen His glory in a death chamber. What a pulpit for the preaching of Jesus is a Christian death-bed!

Is the redeeming Lord hid to you? If He be hid He is hid to them that are perishing. Can it be, shall it be, that you are among that fateful number? Seek ye His face and seek it now. He will not be hid from your eyes if you seek Him truly. O live in the light of His countenance and you shall never die.

XIII

THE CONSISTENCY BETWEEN
CHARACTER AND CONDUCT

"The hireling fleeth because he is an hireling."—JOHN x. 13.

IS not that a very shallow explanation? It reads like an explanation which does not explain. It is as if one said the hero acts heroically because he is a hero, the Christian acts Christianly because he is a Christian. Or, on the sombre side of things, a drunkard drinks because he is a drunkard, or a liar lies because he is a liar. Unphilosophical philosophy! Had any uttered these words save He like whom never man spake we should dismiss them as obviously and pitiably shallow. But we have come to learn —have we not?—that there is never shallowness in the words of Christ. His simplest utterances have the clarity of infinite depth. We are therefore persuaded that, though at first blush our text seems to be no explanation, it really must be a very deep explanation. Let us see.

" The hireling fleeth because he is an hireling."
Is the explanation inadequate ?   Is it superficial ?
The principle of these words is that a man does
what he does because he is what he is.   And
it is to that thought I now call your attention.
Is not that true ?   There is ever a rigid consistency
between character and conduct.   " The hireling
fleeth because he is an hireling."   It is a really
philosophical explanation of the fugitive's deed.
That is the open secret of every man's doings.

The really determining expression of the text
is " because he is."   That settles everything in
your conduct.   Tell me what a man is and I
will tell you what he will do.   The law of inexorable correspondence between the character
and the conduct is a tremendous law.   Conduct
explains manhood.   Always and everywhere and
necessarily a man does what he does because he
is what he is.

So the parallel explanations that also seemed
quite flimsy are far from being such.   A hero
does heroically because he is a hero.   That is so
and must be so.   A man must be a hero before
he can do heroically.   The heroes of our battlefields were heroes long before they saw the battle
field.   Heroism was accumulating within them
from childhood, and when the chance of noble

deeds came they wrought heroically because they were heroes. Character and conduct corresponded.

The Christian acts Christianly because he is a Christian. That proposition is equally valid. There is no deeper explanation of a Christian act. If we are Christian we will infallibly do Christianly. A man is a Christian before he can do a Christian action. Christianity is a renewal of the inward nature, a re-birth of the Spirit. If any man be in Christ he is a new creation, and when the new creation is achieved its effluence, flow forth. Become and you will do.

On the evil side of the case the solemn law applies. The drunkard drinks because he is a drunkard. He is a drunkard before he drinks to excess. Drunkenness is a spirit, a temper, a demon—would God that rampant demon of to-day were exorcised! When the ill opportunity comes the man reveals what he is by what he does. The liar lies because he is a liar. A man is a liar before he tells a lie. Lying is a spirit, a temper, a demon, and the foul influence is in the soul ere the base word leaves the lips. On every side the principle holds good, eternally good. There is perforce a great consistency between character and conduct. The stream attests the fount.

I want to lay repeated emphasis on this. A man does what he does because he is what he is. " The hireling fleeth because he is an hireling." What is a hireling? A man who works for pay? Then we are all hirelings. That is not the sense in which our Lord used the word, nor is it the popular meaning to-day. A hireling is one who works for pay, *and for no other reason.* A hireling is a mercenary. A hireling has no other impulse than the lust of lucre. Always there are the ideas of servility and contemptibleness associated with a hireling. Macaulay could find no stronger phrase by which to dub a certain sort of valour, than " hireling chivalry." The hireling's heart is wrong, therefore his act is wrong. What, under given conditions, can we anticipate of an hireling, but flight? The man does what he does because he is what he is. Let me illustrate this great principle. I know that the reverse is also true—we are what we are because we do what we do—but I desire to ponder the one aspect of the law to-day.

I. Conduct is the Revelation of Character.

" The hireling fleeth because he is an hireling." It was the flight that demonstrated the man.

You might never have known that he was an hireling had he not fled. What I do reveals what I am. An evil heart adumbrates itself in an evil deed. The coward heart shows itself in the fleet foot. The craven scamper tells of the contemptible spirit. Nothing else could reveal the man adequately. There is no infallible test of character except conduct. That is the teaching of Jesus. There is no final and absolute test of Christian character save Christian conduct.

Will not *Christian profession* answer as a sufficient test? Ah no. Christian profession is much to be desired and prized. Very often it is as a sacrament. We must hold it fast. But it is by no means an infallible test of character. It may be the white robe in which a black demon is garbed. Men have professed to be Christ's disciples, and have by their lives blasphemed Him continually. Conduct is the last and solely sure test. By what thou doest thou tellest what thou art.

Is not *the possession of an orthodox Christian creed* an ample test of character?

No. A correct creed is a noble thing, but it is inadequate as a proof of personal godliness. Never listen to those who say it matters not what you believe. It greatly matters. Everywhere a creed is necessary to right conduct. You have a creed as to the ordering of your home and your business. And you have need of a creed in religion. But a man may have a lovely creed, and an unlovely life. A creed is not a certain indication of our character. You may be orthodox as the devil and corrupt as he. Perhaps the most solemn of New Testament writers says, "Thou believest that there is one God; thou doest well. The devils also believe and tremble." A sublime creed the demons have—"There is one God." It is good to have such a creed: "Thou doest well." But it is not enough—hell is orthodox, but it is yet hell. Our creed hardly makes us tremble, but the devils are caused to tremble by their creed, yet the emotion is associated with an incurably evil character. What a warning! Herein lies somewhat of the terribleness of being a Christian—my splendid creed may have its sequel in an impoverished soul. Not my creedal orthodoxy, but my regenerated daily conduct is the conclusive test of my regenerated character. That great truism is the very breath of this text of mine. A man shows what he really is by what he does. Nothing but deeds reveal the innermost essence of mankind.

How do you stand that test? What is the verdict upon you in your home? We know the heart by the conduct. What are you thus shown to be? A man does what he does because he is what he is. Carlyle put it of Alfred Tennyson that he was manufacturing his bit of chaos into cosmos. Can that be said of you? Oh, make it manifest that you are so doing! If your conduct declares your character to be earthly and evil, remember the words of Dean Church, " I can change within, not by necessity, but *by choice*." Make it your choice to change within. " Turn ye, turn ye." By doing righteousness prove that, through the Redeemer's grace, you are righteous.

II. CHARACTER IS REVEALED BY OUR CONDUCT IN THE CRISES OF LIFE.

" The hireling fleeth because he is an hireling." When is it that the hireling fleeth? We have the vivid answer, the allegorical answer, in the twelfth verse, " the hireling seeth *the wolf coming*." Then it is that he reveals how unmistakably he is an hireling, for then it is that " he fleeth." " The wolf coming " discovers the hireling. You might never have known what he was had not the wolf come. His conduct at the tragical crisis manifested his real character.

How that idea of "the wolf" has entered into all literature since Christ employed the symbol! What a contribution the Bible has made to secular literature. The world of figure and parable has been wonderfully enriched by Christ. Macaulay reminded Lady Holland on one occasion that the word "talent" was first used by our Lord in one of His parables. She was quite amazed, though she professed a mastery of literature. And Macaulay says by way of comment, " How absurd for people to profess to have mastered the delicacies of the English language if they do not know the Bible." The contributions of the Son of God to literature are incalculable. We constantly read and speak of "the wolf" as a figure of the great critical hour, the time of disadvantage, and sorrow, and tragedy.

"The wolf coming." It is a wonderful figure by which to represent a crisis of trial or grief, St. Paul afterwards borrowed it from his Lord, and spoke to the Ephesian elders of "grievous wolves." "The wolf coming." Nothing in the allegory is more arresting than this simile.

Now it is that crisis which evokes the conduct

which proves the character. Till the wolf came the "good shepherd" ("the fair shepherd") and the hireling were all but alike and indistinguishable. But the wolf showed which was which, and that immediately and finally. The crises of life reveal the fair shepherds and the hirelings. When the wolf comes "the fair shepherd giveth his life for the sheep." Sacrifice proves fair shepherdliness. But "the hireling fleeth." Selfishness demonstrates hirelinghood.

We really owe an obligation to "the wolf." He decides character for us. He enables us to discriminate. We never know what a soul is till a cruel crisis comes. Suffering reveals the Spirit. What is the man when sorrow comes? When the wolf looms upon him a vision of terror? If a man suffer as a Christian he is a Christian indeed. We never know our moral and spiritual incapacity till sorrow comes. There is a sense in which any man can be good on a sunny day. But the cloudy and dark day reveals "the root of the matter."

Are we full of *fear* when distress approaches? Remember that "the fearful" are doomed at last. Fear is not merely a weakness, it is criminality. Do not coddle yourself because you fear, denounce yourself. "If thou faint in the day of adversity thy strength is small." The day of adversity often declares our feebleness.

Are we *selfish* when sorrow visits us? " The hireling fleeth " when " the wolf cometh." He shows his deplorable selfishness then. He has no thought but self-preservation. He is in his very heart an egoist. It is saddening that sorrow not unfrequently brings out the selfishness of a character. Sorrow does not necessarily effect sanctification. Some men are damned by it. There are those who never show their ingrained selfishness until they are in trouble. Visit such and their one theme is themselves and their griefs. We saw how self-devoted they were when the wolf came. The crisis revealed the character.

Are we *mean* when afflictive circumstances surround us? The hireling fleeing before the wolf is the embodiment of meanness. He dashes away for dear life and forsakes all his duties and responsibilities. The mean side of the nature is often developed amid trials. Men often disappoint God and their fellows in hours of sadness.

Are we *unsympathetic* when sorrow environs us? " The hireling fleeth " when the wolf cometh, and we are told that " he careth not for the sheep." We see his utter lack of sympathy with them when the crisis comes. The awful hours of life

will test our sympathy. Train your sympathies.
" Care for the sheep." The tender and shepherdly
heart will vindicate itself when the cruel wolf
appears upon the scene. The hireling's quality
will clearly show itself then. Pray God that when
life's crises come you may be prepared to abide
the fiery test. What are you like to be manifested
as ? The fair shepherd or the hireling ? That
is the question you are called to face. By the
eternal Spirit's grace keep your heart with all
diligence against the decisive hour. Accept Sir
Thomas Browne's injunction," " Behold *within*
thee the long train of thy trophies, not without
thee."

There are certain testing crises sure to come,
and in these our character will be indisputably
declared. *Temptation* is such a crisis. Who
has not known such a test? It revealed you
—to yourself and perhaps to others. Possibly
you had not long been " in Christ." Many
wondered how you would abide the test. You
were enabled to conquer. You showed, through
grace, the reality of your faith. Henceforth your
calibre is known and approved. Maybe it was
a secret temptation. None saw but God and
yourself. You were sorely tempted. But you
cried, " How shall I do this great wickedness and

sin against the Lord?" You revealed what you are by what you did.

Death is a crisis which manifests character perhaps more distinctly than anything else. That physical change is a great spiritual test. It is a dangerous thing to say as the dying Puritan did, "Come, children, and see how a Christian can die." It is dangerous because it may lead to an attempt to die dramatically. Death is our last great temptation. Satan will turn our dying bed into a stage, and make us actors thereon if he can. No—we would deprecate a dramatic death. But we pray to die a Christian death. A Christian dies well; perhaps not triumphantly, but well. Sure the last end of the good man is peace. We shall know what you really are in that final hour. Masks drop off then. That mysterious crisis has full often shown the grand, sweet reality of Christ's people. Mr. Spurgeon said he had known a husband and wife dying together in the Lord, and they were so rich in grace that they were happier than on their wedding-day. Such miracles of the grace of God do these modern times display.

The Second Advent of our Lord is another crisis which will reveal men. All too rarely do we contemplate this great truth. I believe our Lord's imminent return is one of the most spiritually awakening doctrines of Scripture. It is one of the most central themes of the New Testament. Much of the coldness and unspirituality of the Churches arises from the lapse of this great doctrine. If our Lord were to leave the skies in Second Advent glory to-day what would our condition be? That great and awful crisis would show us as we are. Multitudes of professing Christians would be scared did the trumpet now sound. They would receive the intimation as doom, and not as glad tidings of immortality. Oh, how will it be with us when the Lord cometh? Be it ours to look for Him and to love His appearing, then that final crisis will not be our ruin; it will be glory everlasting.

Prepare ye for life's successive crises by living a life of faith in the Son of God who loved and gave Himself for man. Be ye the Lord's, and under all tests ye shall abide safely.

III. My closing word shall be a word of evangelical appeal. EVANGELICALISM HAS A SOVEREIGN SECRET FOR THE ACHIEVEMENT OF CHARACTER.

The evangelical system secures noble deeds by creating noble souls. The Saviour re-creates the man, and so transfigures the man's conduct. "Ye must be born again." The individual nature must undergo a distinct and radical spiritual change. The condition of such a change is faith or trust in the Son of God, who hath redeemed us unto God by His death. Have you experienced that vital renewal? In such a regeneration lies the spring of morality. Transform the heart by the power of God's Spirit, and inevitably you transform the deed. Lovely souls do lovely deeds. Be a Christian and you will act as a Christian.

Again and again evangelicalism has proved itself the inspiration of beautiful works, having first beautified the doer of the works. The examples are innumerable. I will now adduce but one. Frank Crossley, of Manchester, was a commercial St. Francis. He surrendered his splendid mansion, and went with his like-minded wife to reside in rooms adjoining a Mission Hall he had built in one of the dreariest parts of Manchester. There he lived the remainder of his consecrated days. Frank Crossley was a magistrate of Manchester, and one day when he sat on the bench a poor Salvation Army girl was brought into the dock and charged with obstructing the thoroughfare by holding a meeting. The moment she appeared Frank Crossley left his seat on the bench and walked into the dock and took his stand by her till the trial was over!

That was sublime! That was a high poetic deed! That is the type of man the Saviour can make! Frank Crossley did what he did because he was what he was.

XIV

THE REPUTATION OF GOD

"And it shall be to the Lord for a name."—IsA. lv. 13.

THE great final issue of redemption is to be
the reputation of God. That is the goal
of all religious achievement. That is the glorious
climax of all things. God shall have a universal
and glorious and everlasting reputation. "It shall
be to Jehovah for a name."

This term "name" is very modern. We are
to-day accustomed to speak of reputation under
the designation of "a name." Here is another
illustration of the modernness of Scripture even
in its literary aspects. We often say, "That man
has a great name," when our reference is to his
far-reaching reputation. Sometimes we use the
expression admonitorily, as when we say, "If you
do not take care you will get your name up."
But by "a name" we mean a reputation. This
Old Testament word carries the same signification
in my text.

By "a name" is here meant a glorious re-presentation of character. This is the Lord's inheritance in the peoples of the earth. His omnipotent force is to forge a name. The splendid issue of man's salvation is to be the reputation of God.

We find God's reputation described as God's "name" otherwhere in the Bible. An impressive instance occurs in the record of Joshua. When Israel was defeated by the men of Ai, Joshua pleaded and remonstrated with the Lord, and dared to say, " What wilt Thou do unto Thy Great Name ? " He dreaded that God's reputation should lose its exceeding lustre. Happy the man in whose soul there surges that sacred dread !

Let us ponder some features of the reputation of God.

I. It is Necessary that God should have a Name.

The prophecy of the text represents an eternal necessity. It is surely righteous that God should have a name. Do we not often forget this ? It is not necessary that we should have a name, but it is obviously necessary that God should. We are in danger of so seeking our individual or ecclesiastical reputation that we forget the reputation of God. We hear much of the rights of man. Would we might hear more concerning the rights of God. Is there not a peril of our forgetting the individuality of God? God's individuality involves individual rights. And God's rights are the supreme rights. One of God's earliest rights is the right of reputation. This right shall be accorded Him, says my text, " And it shall be to the Lord for a name."

God desires a name. Some believe in an impassive God. Surely not such is the God of the Bible. God has His feelings. God has His personal desires. And He desires a reputation widespread and splendid. But He does not desire it for His own sake alone. Far more does He enjoin it for His people's sake. It is necessary God should have a name that His people may realize it. One of our greatest spiritual blessings is to realize the reputation of God. Theology is concerned with God's reputation. How can the reputation of God be augmented without a great theology? For this reason we need more theological preaching and teaching. Men must know what God is that they may appreciate Him with reverent appreciation. Do you realize God's fragrant reputa-

tion? It is your finest sacrament? Do you
realize that God's reputation grows grander as
the days pass by? Do you spread that reputation
in your family, among your servants, among your
friends? In giving God a name you are getting
to yourself a great reward. To extend God's
reputation is to be enriched with great enrich-
ment.

It is necessary God should have a name for
the world's sake. Man, considered as separated
from God by sin, needs to know that august
and redeeming name. Go and tell the sinning
hosts of earth what a God is our God! Tell
them He is as great in tenderness as in power!
Tell them God is love, not merely that He is
loving, but that He is love! Give God a name,
for till men know God they are dead whilst they
live. Oh, how the world needs to hear of God!
The greatest service we can render to humanity
is to give our God a name. Tell them what He
is, and you shall lure them to Him. It appears,
then, that the reputation of God is a manifold
necessity: for His own sake, for His people's
sake, and for man's sake is the word of prophecy
written, "And it shall be to the Lord for a
name."

Thank God for His "name"! Countless

millions adore Him.   Millions of regenerated men
would die for Him.   He is the life of life to
innumerable multitudes.   " Like fragrance on the
breezes His name abroad is poured."   What
would the world be without the name of God
which echoes through it!   Let that ineffable
reputation fill and overflow the universe!   The
supreme need of the years is that God be all in
all.   The prophecy of the text is deeply grounded
in the nature of things.   " And it shall be to
the Lord for a name."   It shall be because it
must be.

II. GOD'S DELIVERANCES OF HIS PEOPLE
GIVE HIM A NAME.

Note the prophecy in ver. 12, " For ye shall go
out . . . and be led forth."   Where from?   From
Babylon.   Where to?   To the homeland.   God
Himself will bring His people out from the house
of bondage.   He will lead them forth from the
scene of their expatriation.   And He will conduct
them to the fatherland, to the old home of
freedom.   Out of the captivity of Babylon into the
enfranchisement of the home-country ; out of the
land of idolatry and sin into the Holy Land,
the land of God.   " Ye shall go out."   What an
exodus !   " And be led forth."   What divine

guidance! You are in captivity now, you and your children. But you shall be delivered, and God Himself shall deliver you. And the glory of your emancipation shall all belong to God. The world shall hear of your deliverance, the world shall be thrilled with God's reputation. "And it shall be to the Lord for a name."

God has a wondrous reputation in all things. But that He is the God of deliverances gives Him His greatest name. What a sublime conception of deliverance God has! "For My thoughts are not your thoughts, neither are your ways My ways, saith the Lord." And wherein lies the disparity? In elevatedness, in magnificence of scale. "For as the heavens are higher than the earth, so are My ways higher than your ways, and My thoughts than your thoughts." All God's thoughts and ways immeasurably exceed ours, but His thoughts and ways regarding salvation or deliverance peculiarly transcend those of men. God has such a conception of redemption as never entered into the heart of man. None of us can fully realize the redeeming power of God. "For ye shall go out . . . and be led forth." What wonderful deliverance God has wrought for His people! "And it shall be to the Lord for a name." Nebuchadnezzar, one of the most weird

characters of the Old Testament, bore a grand
witness to God's delivering power. I wish we
were all as frank and open to conviction as was
he. He said, "There is no God that can deliver
after this sort." Do you whom God has signally
delivered bear as clear a testimony? Do you, in
this matter, give God a name?

God delivers from *guilt*. Do not let that doctrinal
word drop out of your religious speech. And
do not make light of the experience. The sense
of guilt is, I fear, diminished in our day. But
if it be so it is to our incalculable loss. Guilt
is the liability to suffer punishment for sin. The
whole world is not only sinful, it is thereby guilty
before God. You once knew the terror of
conscious guilt. Like Newman, you were terrified
at yourself. You were scared at the vision of
your accountability. But God has delivered you.
He said to you in your distress, "Ye shall go
out . . . and be led forth." And He was equal to
His clement word. He showed you the way of
deliverance. You saw that *your* sins were laid
on Jesus His Son. You realised that you need
bear them no more. You entered into the
evangelical rapture of knowing that the Saviour
loved *you* and gave Himself for you. The terror
of guilt died away. You outsoared it at the

cross. Out of Babylon our redeeming God led you into the land of liberty. Have you given God a name? Do you tell men that the Lord, and He alone, led you forth? Shame on the redeemed soul that gives no name to the God of his redemption! Oh, tell men what has been done for you, and who He is that has done it. Be we all fulfillers of this prophecy, "It shall be to the Lord for a name." The fact, the experimental and the scientific fact, that you have left your guilt behind must be used to spread far and wide the reputation of God.

God delivers from *evil habit*. He not only cancels past guilt but averts new guilt. He gives supernatural power, even the power of His own personal Spirit, to enable against sin. This is an actual experience in the lives of men. Long some of us were held in the Babylon of sin. We sought deliverance by our own arm, but utterly failed. We looked to our fellow-men, but in them there was no help. At length God said, " Ye shall go out . . . and be led forth." We believed His word of grace, and we have experienced the great spiritual deliverance. We have turned our back on our bondage. It is a matter of fact. The proof is in our character. The evidence is palpable in our consciousness and in our daily

life. Do we give God a name for it? Oh, let
others know where alone such deliverance can
be found. It shall be the healing of the nations
that they hear of God's redeeming name.

God delivers from *sorrow*. We have mourned
in the strange land of grief. By the rivers of
Babylon we have sat down and wept. Rivers
of tears have flowed into the rivers of Babylon.
But God spake to our sorrowful souls and said,
" Ye shall go out . . . and be led forth." A great
deliverance He gave us. Again and again and
again He has done it. And for hosts of His
people has He wrought wondrous emancipations.
"This is the Lord's doing, and it is marvellous
in our eyes." Proclaim it everywhere. It is
criminal silence if we decline to declare God's
deliverances. Trust in Him, ye people. God is
the delivering God. Spread His fame abroad.
Seeing He has brought you forth from bondage,
see to it that it be to the Lord for a name.

III. The Characteristics of God's People
Give Him a Name.

The emancipated ones are to be marked by
"joy" and "peace" (ver. 12). These features are
to grace them at the great crisis of their
deliverance, and also in the ordinary life they

lead on their return to their own country. And this shall extend God's reputation. "It shall be to the Lord for a name."

They were not to come out of bondage hanging their heads, but lifting them up with triumphant joy, and assuring their hearts with serenest peace. No haunting memories and no stinging fears! "Ye shall go out with joy and be led forth with peace." God enhances His fame by clothing His people with such royal vesture.

We give God a name when gracious characteristics mark us. Joy is the privilege of the Lord's redeemed. "Rejoice in the Lord alway; and again I say rejoice" is the Apostle's word. How full of meaning is that insistent, "again I say"! But let the Apostle stand aside and hear the Master. "These things have I spoken unto you, that your joy might be full." An affluent joy is the guerdon Jesus brings to His people even in this life. And what reflects such honour upon God as a joyous Christian?

But peace is an even richer gift. The restless world needs peace above all else to-day, for a great unrest is at the heart of things. God promises to lead His people forth with peace. Day by day and hour by hour in all your journeyings, and then in the final journey, "ye shall be led forth with peace." Even when you grow old and weak, and the life-day declines, still with peace shall you pursue your appointed way. Ruskin reminds us in his " Crown of Wild Olive " that Friedrich, the hereditary name of the German princes, meant " rich in peace." That is the hereditary nature of all the children of God.

If we had more manifest peace and joy, what a name it would be for God! Men always think more highly of God when they see these qualities in His people. God's reputation is largely dependent upon the characteristics of His followers. Our poverty of character clouds His fair name. Be our constant endeavour so to adorn God's teaching as to replenish His reputation. Walk worthily of the Lord. Our lives are the only theology most men will read. Be we jealous to give the world an adequate and lovely impression of God. Let our joy and peace be now, and to life's latest hour, to the Lord for a name.

IV. NATURE, AS SUGGESTIVE OF THE SPIRITUAL, GIVES GOD A NAME.

" For ye shall go out with joy, and be led forth with peace." And will Nature be wholly or partially unsympathetic ? By no means. " The mountains and the hills shall break forth before you into singing, and all the trees of the field shall clap their hands."

Nature has a mystical value. Mountains, hills, and trees reveal to the devout soul a spiritual sympathy. The Creation is tremulous with the Creator. When men discern the spiritual element in Nature it is to the Lord for a name.

To some souls Nature is non-spiritual. They find God eludes them in that province. To others Nature is a shrine of God and is crammed with heaven. Blessed are they who find a spiritual suggestion in Nature. More blessed they who discover a responsiveness in Nature to their great spiritual experiences. "Let him that heareth understand." There are, thank God, a host of mystic believers who know what it is as God leads them forth to find that the mountains and hills break forth before them into singing, and all the trees of the field clap their hands When Nature is seen to suggest the spiritual it is indeed to the Lord for a name.

Do you see the spiritual in Nature? Sir Thomas Browne said, "We must not disdain to suck divinity from the flowers of Nature." The flowers of Nature are full of divinity. And it wonderfully adds to the reputation of God when this is seen to be so. All that helps men to

realize Nature as a vast spiritual suggestion infallibly is to the Lord for a name.

Said Blake, who was alike painter and poet,
" You ask me if, when I look at the sunrise, I
see a round disc of fire something like a guinea.
No, I do not. I see an innumerable company of
the heavenly host, crying, ' Holy, Holy, Holy.' " He
added, " I look through the window not with it."
A noble testimony ! Such a testimony is to the
Lord for a name. Can you bear similar witness ?

They who look on Nature with purged eyes
see in mountains, and hills, and trees, and all
things a spiritual suggestion. They gather eternal
parables from temporal objects. When God leads
them the mountains and hills break forth before
them into singing, and all the trees of the field
clap their hands.

Tell men of Nature's spiritual content and
response. Cause men to see God in everything.
Make them to know that Nature's great idea
is spiritual. Thus will you be continually
honoured to add to God's reputation. " It shall
be to the Lord for a name."

V. ALL BEAUTIFUL TRANSFORMATIONS GIVE
GOD A NAME.

" Instead of the thorn shall come up the fir-tree,

and instead of the brier shall come up the myrtle-tree : and it shall be to the Lord for a name." Perhaps the " it " carries this as the chief idea, though it refers, as we have sought to show, to the subject-matter of vers. 12 and 13.

What is the ultimate meaning of the great transformation here predicted ? I think it could hardly be stated more clearly than in the words of a Jewish annotator, " Instead of the wicked shall rise up the righteous, and instead of the transgressor men that fear sin." Such noble transformations shall give to God a yet more splendid renown.

Personal conversion ever adds to the reputation divine. When the individual " thorn " becomes a " fir-tree," and the individual " brier " is metamorphosed into a " myrtle-tree," it is by the power of God alone, and how signally it redounds to God's honour ! To transform the repellant into the attractive and the injurious into the beneficent, this is the crowning work of God. Has He thus transformed you ? Then your regenerated character is to the Lord for a name. Men shall celebrate a God who can work such wonders. We have frequent and arresting evidence that nothing gives God such fame as individual conversion. Every renewed nature is a testimony to God. No instrument sounds forth "Hallelujah to the Lord" like a regenerated life. It is to the Lord for a name.

What a name God already has by means of transformations He has wrought on character! Have *you* given Him a name? Does your changed life speak His immortal renown?

National and world-wide conversion will glorify God's reputation in inconceivable degree. When everywhere, "instead of the thorn shall come up the fir-tree, and instead of the brier shall come up the myrtle-tree," what a name shall Jehovah have! Is not this a ruling argument for world evangelization? It may well fire us with evangelistic zeal that wherever men's lives are transformed God's reputation is made more glorious. We love dear friends to have a name, and shall we not desire far more earnestly a name for our God? Oh, spread the gospel of the Son of God everywhere. Loyally and sacrificingly sustain those who are spreading it; be fellow-evangelists with them. So when earth's thorns become fir-trees, and earth's briers become myrtle-trees, and God's name is thus everywhere glorious, you shall have the joy of having laboured toward that golden consummation.

"It shall be to the Lord for a name." It is,

our obligation and privilege to seek to fulfil that glowing word of prophecy. God's reputation in great degree rests with us. God help us to guard well the inestimable deposit. Shall not we, in His Spirit, nerve ourselves to achieve this splendid issue? To make God's reputation ever more widespread and ever more illustrious—this is a task heaven's brightest angels might covet most.

Perish all mean, selfish ambitions in the sublime service of the world's salvation! "It shall be to the Lord for a name." Be this our one object and aim! There is no room for lesser motives. At the Saviour's cross all other motives die.

"It shall be to the Lord for a name." A saved world will give to this prophecy its transcendent fulfilment. When it shall be, and how it shall be, who can say? But to this splendid end let us consecrate our every power. To give God a name let us be willing to live and die.

XV

THE NEARNESS OF CHRIST

"The Lord is at hand."—PHIL. iv. 5.

A BRIEF and pregnant message! It is even
more compacted as Paul utters it. What
he literally said was, "The Lord near." Three
words! No verb was used, for none was needed.
It is abrupt to the point of dramatism. It is a
bolt of benediction.

And is it not good news? To know that life's
highest good is "at hand" is verily a gospel.
Christ is here, as always in the New Testament,
"the Lord." To be assured that He is "at hand"
or "near" is to have a great calm amid the storm
of life. So often the things we most desiderate
are remote. How much we hear of "disillusion-
ment" in these days! And truly the most delectable benisons seem often to recede with the years.
The fortune you have looked for and struggled
after. Is it "at hand"? Ah me, no! It is as
if it vanished into greater distance as you pursue

it. But "the Lord is *at hand*"! The culture you have sought so laboriously. It grows to your disappointed consciousness painfully remote. But "the Lord is *at hand*"! The very love you have inquired for these stony years passes further and further into remoteness. But "the Lord is *at hand*"! Life's noblest possibility and greatest blessedness is within reach of us each. There is no mocking distance between it and you. The most precious is the most near. "The Lord is at hand!"

It was this truth which gave urgency and charm to the preaching of our Lord's forerunner. "Repent ye," cried the mighty and gracious Baptist, "for the kingdom of heaven is at hand." John summoned the multitude to a spiritual good which was not remote but near. Our Lord's first public message was moulded on that of His harbinger, "Repent ye, for the kingdom of heaven is *at hand.*" To a near, an ever-available blessedness Christ called the sad and sinful sons of men. To that same immediacy of good Paul directs the minds and hearts of the Philippians when he exclaims, "The Lord is at hand." Christianity is a present salvation.

The stress of the message is in the words, one word on the pen of Paul—"at hand," or "near."

What does it mean? Does it refer to Christ's imminence or to His Second Advent? The word may carry either reference. And our best interpreters have agreed that this is so, and have only differed as to which is the predominant idea. Calvin, the prince of the commentators, prefers the thought of Christ's present contiguity. So does Bishop Moule, who describes this as "the leading truth of the text." So does Dean Vaughan, who had such wondrous insight into Scripture teaching. Whilst such teachers as Dean Alford, and Meyer, and Bishop Lightfoot prefer the eschatological interpretation of this terse and stirring watchword. We shall do well to read the text as bearing to us the dual message.

I. "THE LORD IS AT HAND" LOCALLY.

Christ was incarnate here, and is now incarnate in heaven, but He is imminent here still. He is "near." His traces are everywhere, and everywhere luminous. He impinges upon us perpetually. Like an atmosphere He pervades this universe. "Thou art near, O Lord," sang the Psalmist, and St. Paul echoes and glorifies the ancient song. Christ said, "I go away and come again," and He has been as good as His word.

Christ is "at hand" in *Nature*. His is the

presence deeply interfused in Creation. " All things were made by Him," and all things are full of Him. He is localized in this vale of time. There is a " Higher Pantheism" of which Tennyson so nobly sang. The Lord is not all things, but He is in all things. "The Lord is at hand." He dwells in every radiant star. He gleams and glows in the sunshine. He tabernacles in the apocalyptic clouds. He dwells in every flower that blows. He is the life and wealth and beauty of Nature. Nature is thrilled with a supernatural presence. Jesus is imminent in Nature. Creation gains its grandeur and songfulness from the indwelling Saviour. We need to realize the cosmic Christ more vividly. Then all earth becomes a temple, and we gladly sing, " The Lord is in His holy temple." Thus to know His immanence is to find Nature rich in spiritual ministries. Amid the grandeurs of winter say ye, " The Lord is at hand." Amid the pageantry of summer cry, " The Lord is at hand." Go forth into the garden, the park, the fields, avowing that "The Lord is at hand." Hear Him in every song that every song-bird sings. Know that He thrills every atom of this visible globe. " By Him all things consist" (hold to-gether). It is a scientific fact that Christ is the centre of Creation. Behold Nature with this master-light. Say, "This is none other than the house of God, and this is the gate of heaven." So shall earth be a sacred place to your reverent consciousness and to your grateful heart. They enter into the Paradise of Nature who can say, "The Lord is at hand" therein. The world means intensely and means good. Nature is the shrine of Jesus.

In *human nature* "the Lord is at hand." There is a word in the incomparable prologue of St. John's incomparable gospel that I sometimes think many of us are afraid of—"The true light which lighteth every man that cometh into the world." There is something of Jesus in every man that is born into the world. A ray of the light divine is in each man constitutionally. We often remark that there is something good in every man. That "something good" is the something of Jesus in every man. Man at birth is "totally depraved," say the theologians; but orthodox theologians have never meant by that that man is as bad as he could be, else man would a devil. Every part of man's nature is depraved, but there is a prevenient grace at work therein. "The true light lighteth every man." If there were not something of Christ in all men, all men would not be salvable. This by no means does away with the necessity of conversion, it makes conversion possible. Naturally there is but a gleam of the true light in man; conversion broadens out the gleam into a splendid meridian. God would have nothing to work on if the Lord were not at hand in human nature. Let all Christian teachers and workers recognise the immanence of Jesus in men. Let them take hopeful views of those whom they seek that they may save. Human nature is the shrine of Jesus.

"The Lord is at hand in *human history*." He is localized there. History overflows with the presence of Jesus. This is the profoundest philosophy of history. This is the secret of all events. Read the history of the English people, and in that history as truly as in the history of Israel, the Lord is at hand. And what is true of such history is quite as true of individual history. Your biography rightly read is a wondrous illustration of the nearness of Christ. What is the moral of your life-story? "The Lord is at hand." The very sorrows and mistakes and sins of our lives are made contributory to our blessedness. By the ministry of chequered experiences the immanent Lord works out His purposes. He causes them to "ripen fast, unfolding every hour." He consummates our character by all we pass through. History is the shrine of Jesus.

Where else is the Lord " at hand " ? Emphatically in *the Bible*. It is the most remarkable illustration of the localization of Jesus. Wondrous word of God ! There is a crowd of evidences of the divinity of this book which is many yet one. But I think the supreme evidence of its inspiration is that here " the Lord is at hand." This is the crowning proof. I despise none of the arguments for the inspiration of the Bible, but increasingly this is to me *the* argument. In every part of this Book I find my near Lord. In every separate book of the Bible I discover that " the Lord is at hand." The saints have always found the Saviour immanent in every portion of the precious volume. In even the books which unspiritual critics dub uninspired or declare to be void of divine revelation. In such books as Esther and the Song of Songs, when rightly read, " the Lord is at hand." This is the touchstone to apply to the Bible as a whole and to its separate books. It will in all its parts abide the test. Do not forget that it is the Christian consciousness, and not scholarship, which has to pronounce the final verdict on the Scriptures.

The faith is delivered not to the *literati*, or to the scientists, or to the philosophers, or to the scholars as such, but to " the saints." Sanctity, not erudition, is the ultimate arbiter. Is not Jesus immanent throughout the Bible? This is the glory of the Book. This proves it the Book of God. Scripture is the shrine of Jesus.

" The Lord is at hand " *in the Christian Church.* He dwells among the believing host as He does not otherwhere. That is the true high churchmanship. And the greatest ideal of the Church is that Christ should so manifestly possess the Church that the awe-struck world will fall down and confess that God is in it of a truth. Give us a Church so evidently filled with Jesus that men shall say, " We must associate ourselves with them if we would find the Lord to be at hand," and such churchmanship can never be overthrown. A spiritual Church is a royal Church. The true Christian Church is the shrine of Jesus.

" The Lord is at hand " *in the Individual Christian.* That is your attainable ideal, Christian man. " Christ in you." The Lord's real presence may be sweetly obvious in you, music on your tongue, kindness in your heart and hands, broadness and tolerance and generosity in your mind. The Lord may be palpitatingly near in you, so that those

around shall know that to be near the Lord they
have only to be near you. Oh for a sweet, mystical
identification between the Lord and the believer !
Oh for an interblending of personality ! Oh to bring
the Lord near to others—in our homes, in business,
in the Church, wherever o'er the plains of time we
wander !

May the immanence of the Saviour, be the
strength and beauty of our lives !

II. " THE LORD IS AT HAND " ACCESSIBLY.

Does not this follow ?   If Jesus Christ be immanent surely He will be accessible ?   And such He
is.   The Psalmist cried, " The Lord is nigh unto
all that call upon Him."   Here again the New
Testament echoes the Old Testament.   The Lord
is always nigh to every one.   But in a very
distinctive sense He is nigh to them that call
upon Him.   Many are near locally who are not
near accessibly.   Some are sympathetically remote
who are locally quite close to us.   Jesus is as near
in helpfulness as in geography.   He is " at hand."
I have His ear, for I have His heart.   He will
hear me when I cry to Him.   A distant Lord
would depress and distress us.   An unapproachable
Saviour would not save us.   But Christ is ever

accessible! I can come to Him when I will and am sure of His kindly relief.

Continually I may prove the accessibility of Christ. In the busy day and in the silent night. In prayer spoken or silent, formal or informal. In Bible-reading. In holy meditation. Ever may we approach our Lord and find a welcome divinely kind.

Ceremonially I may prove my Lord's accessibility. " The Lord is at hand " is the deepest meaning of all religious ceremony and its highest blessedness. It is not essential that our ceremonialism be of any particular type. Some profit by an ample ceremony. Some need only the simplest ceremony. The degree is of little moment. That may well be left to individual or congregational preference. In all such matters let there be wide liberty. But some ceremonialism all must have. Our faith needs to fix itself to form. And the test of all rites and ceremonies is, do they bring to my experience the near Christ? Can I say as I engage therein, " The Lord is at hand ? " Elaborate ceremony without the Lord at hand is a decorated delusion. Simplest ritual if the Lord be at hand is precious as preciousness itself. Is the Lord evidently "at hand" in our acts of worship? Grand or austere, blessed is the worship

wherein the soul says, " The Lord is at hand." That
was a God-breathed sermon which made you say,
" The Lord is at hand."   Test all ceremony by this
rule.   Elevate all   worship   to   this celestial
standard.

In the exigencies of life " the Lord is at hand."
The Psalmist anticipated this truth again. He sang,
" The Lord is nigh unto them that are of a broken
heart."   Have you never been writ down in that
pathetic category, " Them that are of a broken
heart " ?   I have.   Who has not known the distressful mystery of a broken heart !   Perchance, as Sir
Walter Scott said of his early heart-brokenness,
your heart has been " handsomely pieced again."
But you have not forgotten that dolorous experience.
The Lord was " at hand " then.   Happy you if you
proved it.   " God is a very present help in time
of trouble."   Who has not, however sunshiny
their life, broken-hearted moods and moments ?
Supremely in those tragic experiences " the
Lord is at hand."   Oh the balmy consolation of
this message !   Will you take this thought with
you into the sorrows of the future ?   Young man,
if to-morrow some awful temptation should en-
thral you ; if the cruel iron hand should be
upon your neck before you know where you
are ; if you should be " *overtaken* in a fault "

—oh, remember to your immediate salvation that "the Lord is at hand." Cry unto Him and He will deliver thee.

Should some sudden sorrow swoop down upon you like a bird of prey, and fix its relentless talons in your quivering flesh, in that extremity of agony remember that "the Lord is at hand." Cry unto Him, and He will deliver thee either from thy trouble or *in* thy trouble. If some overwhelming conviction of sin rush upon thee, and thou art ready to perish with dismay, "the Lord is at hand." Lay thy sins upon Him. Thy redeeming Lord shall prove Himself near to thine uplifting.

Except the Lord come, the last great exigency will erewhile come upon us all. We shall be face to face with what men call death. Then be our consolation this, that "the Lord is at hand." He is never nearer to His people than in the final hour. Commit thy spirit, then, to His care, and we shall hear the sweet swan-song, "I will fear no evil, for Thou art with me."

Praised be the ever-accessible Christ! He is most to His people when they need Him most. He is a friend in need; the sole friend in life's extremest needs. "Speak to Him, then, for He hears." Such a Lord is Lord indeed. He must be a divine Saviour whose help is so constant and universal.

III. "THE LORD IS AT HAND" ESCHATO-LOGICALLY.

Not only is Christ ever imminent, He is coming in the clouds of heaven. And His coming is no remote event. He is travelling earthwards fast. Soon He will appear in His glory. Very real to the early Christians was the Lord's return. He Himself declared it in no equivocal terms. His proclamation of His Second Advent hastened His shameful death. They hurried Him to Calvary when they heard His sure prophetic word concerning His glorious return. What a place the Second Advent has in the New Testament! Positively no other doctrine is so much alluded to. It colours the Book. This message of my text is very characteristic of apostolic teaching. "The Lord is at hand." This, says Bishop Light-foot, is "the Apostle's watchword." "Maranatha," the Aramaic equivalent, is a solemn word which throws its shadow over Paul's letter to the Corinthian Christians.

Oh, what a truth is this, "the Lord is at hand" If He were "at hand" centuries ago, how much more is He "at hand" now! The Lord may at any time appear. He may come to-day! In the silence and gloom of midnight His trumpet may sound and His awful glory blaze upon us!

Do we love His appearing? Are we looking for our Lord? Is it a solemn joy, a strength in service, a consolation in sorrow, a hope for the sinful world, that " the Lord is at hand"?

Strange it is that this paramount truth of Scripture is so neglected in the Churches of to-day. How little is the proclamation heard, " The Lord is at hand"! Sure I am that the apathy concerning this theme is a master-achievement of Satan. It is a device of the devil that we have so lost the proportion of the faith. Of things of which Scripture says little we say much, and of things of which the oracles of God say much we are all but silent. It is a victory of the evil one in the Church of Christ. Almost above all other truths Satan detests that of the Lord's Second Coming. Where it is believed and taught there is fervent spirituality, evangelistic zeal, and foreign missionary passion. Nothing so quickens the life and service of God's people as does a realization of the nearness of the Lord's return. And to prevent this Satan has blinded the eyes of too many in the modern Church. I pray that the Spirit of God will open the eyes that are holden. How we need a deep spirituality in the Churches! To know that "the Lord is at hand" will infallibly secure the highest good. Out of this all blessedness will spring.

Awake ye to this glorious truth, ye servants of God! Christ is coming visibly, personally, to take to Himself His great power and reign. Are we looking for Him? I fear that did He come to-day full many a professing Christian would be thankful to any rock or hill in their neighbourhood that would fall on them and hide them from the face of the Judge. But His eyes of flame pierce all rocks and hills.

Be we ready when He shall come. Let the Lord's Second Advent nearness tell upon our lives. The text is used as an argument for forbearance or gentleness. "Let your forbearance (marg. R.V. gentleness) be known unto all men. The Lord is at hand."

Yes. That is the conclusion of the whole matter. The return of our Lord viewed as near should make us rich in Christian character. What manner of persons ought we to be who believe that "the Lord is at hand"? *That* is the vital consideration. The Lord's coming should make us like unto Him for whom we look.

XVI

LOWERING THE SEA

"King Ahaz took down the sea from off the brasen oxen that were under it, and put it upon a pavement of stones."—2 KINGS xvi. 17.

WHAT does that matter to us? It is ages since this sacrilege was wrought. Yes. But there is no ancient history in the Bible. The anciency only appertains to the drapery of these old records, the principles are eternal.

Our deeds may have been apparently very remote from the mad deed of King Ahaz, and yet we may have done substantially the same thing.

"King Ahaz . . . took down the sea." The reference is to the enormous and superb laver which was sitnate in the temple, and was intended for the cleansing of the priests. In 1 Kings vii. 23-27 the magnificent laver is fully described. It is there termed "the molten sea." Why was it called a sea? for the expression is suggestive of Oriental exaggeration. The Hebrew word for a sea is not confined in its use to the ocean, but is applied to any body of water. It is applied in the Old Testament to rivers. The Nile and the Euphrates are so described. This laver of the temple was called a sea because of its immense capacity. Josephus says "its figure was that of an hemisphere."

Bowls of considerable size were not uncommon in Assyria, nor are references to such bowls wanting in Greek and Roman history. But never was there one on the scale of this "sea." It was fifteen feet in diameter at the top. It was forty-seven feet in circumference. It was seven and a half feet in depth. The "sea" must have bulged considerably below the brim if it, held two thousand "baths," for the bath was the largest liquid measure among the Hebrews. The bottom of this sea rested on the backs of brasen oxen whose hinder parts were inwards.

The "sea" was set for a sign in the Temple of Jehovah, and assuredly the sacrilegious icono-clasm of Ahaz is significant for us with manifold significance.

I. We have not lowered the sea! No. *But we have frustrated the divine plan.* That plan we may not have spoiled utterly, thanks to restraining grace, but we have frustrated it in detail. The molten sea represented a divine plan. God was the architect. This is true of every detail of this sea. God directed its dimensions. Every inch of it was planned of Almighty wisdom. Its design in every particular was God's work. The lily-like shape of the brim, the thickness of the metal, the pose of the brasen oxen—all in minutest detail was divinely planned. True, Ahaz did not frustrate God's plan as a whole. He was restrained from going to extremest lengths of desecration. He did not smash up the sea into atoms. He did not pulverize it. But he spoiled it in its detail. He "took down the sea from off the brasen oxen that were under it, and put it upon a pavement of stones." He put it out of its right relations. He threw it out of plumb. He lowered its level. He ruined its genius.

Everything is divinely planned. There is a Providence of detail, a theology of trifles. It looks as if there might be much in Plato's idea that all earthly things have their perfect forms in heaven. But oh, how men have frustrated the celestial plan! Not entirely, but as to its detail. We have lowered the sea which we have not been permitted to destroy. We have a fatal faculty for lowering levels and altering relations for the worse. A monkey can spoil the invention which genius has devised. An infant can wreck what industrious skill has created. A careless servant has burnt a manuscript over which a mighty intellect has laboured long. Construction is difficult, destruction is easy. And oh, how men have put out their hands to the task of frustrating the beauteous details of the divine plan of things. King Ahaz did once what we are continually doing.

Have we not frustrated the divine plan? Look at the *material world*. Is it to-day as God designed it? Nature is "red in tooth and claw with ravin." "The whole creation groaneth and travaileth." Man has spoiled God's plan. *Commerce* is not to-day as divinely instituted. God never intended business to be a game of grab, a struggle wherein one man clutches another by the throat. It was surely not God's idea that business should coarsen and corrupt those who engage in it. Ah, how men have impaired the divine plan of commerce!

We have dealt similarly with *the home*. Is home life, in many cases, according to the plan of heaven? It is too often a scene of selfishness, an arena for all manner of petty contentions. Some homes are almost hells. Great God ! how we have frustrated the pattern Thou didst design ! The noble institution of the home is not effaced, but many of its fairest qualities are lacking through man's evil spoliation.

A similar remark applies to *the Church.* Thanks be to God, the heaven-ordained corporation abides. But is it as God meant it to be ? Our sectarian exclusiveness, our uncharitable orthodoxies, our jealousies, our impious calmness whilst men die in darkness all around us—are these things such as God approves ? We have here again repeated the folly of King Ahaz and impaired the detail of God's plan.

And is not this conspicuously applicable to *our individuality* ? Sovereign and restraining grace have kept us from self-destruction, but we have sadly marred ourselves. Some of us have deteriorated with amazing deterioration. The most fine gold is dimmed almost unrecognizably. In this and that feature of our character we are perverted. We have almost unmade ourselves. Friend, pause in thy suicidal course. Stop and think and repent. Thy soul, like the natural sea and the molten sea of the ancient temple, is God's, and He made it. Beware of counter-

working God's working.   No longer emulate the
deed of Ahaz, who "took down the sea from off
the brasen oxen that were under it, and put
it upon a pavement of stones."

II. We have not lowered the sea! No. *But
we have maimed good and useful things.* Again
I say Ahaz did not destroy the sea.   He, however,
sadly interfered with its utility.   It is a moot
point whether he did not render it all but useless.
Remember the sea existed for the cleansing of the
priests.   If, as many think, the water flowed from
the sea through the mouths of the brasen oxen,
then by placing it on a pavement of stones Ahaz
rendered it well-nigh ineffective.   The cleansing
of the priests was a less easy task by reason of
the King's wild wicked deed.

A parable indeed !   Man ever and again maims
what is good and useful in its operation.   " Who
did hinder ? " inquires the Apostle.   It is generally
a " who " rather than a " what."   Persons, not
things, are the accustomed hinderers.   The history
of man is a history of maiming.   Often men have
hindered when they should have helped what is good
and true and holy.   Thus *the Bible* has often been
treated.   Its supernatural elements have been
discounted.   Its evangelicalism has been belittled.

Its ethics have been decried. Some have sought to evacuate it of its inspiration, and so to degrade it into a common book.

The Sabbath is subjected to a similar process. Its warrant is questioned. Its sanctity is doubted. Its claims are slighted, if not ridiculed.

Worship is maimed by methods close akin to those just indicated. How often it is materialized. Instead of being spiritual it is dramatic. Rather than an inspiration to service, it is too often a selfish luxury. It is a fashion where it ought to be a sacrifice, a display where it should be an agony.

Society is not exempted from spoliative influences. Society was designed to be a grand brotherhood and sisterhood. A solidarity of love and sympathy. But, generally speaking, is it so? Alas no: it is almost the antithesis of this. It abounds in cruel selfishness. It is rank with inconsiderateness. It is hollow with heartlessness. It is gaudy with self-display.

Verily King Ahaz when he maimed the good and useful " sea " but dimly parabolized the crowds of his successors in these latter days.

Worse than all else, many of us have maimed our souls. We have inflicted deadly injury on our characters ; we have made havoc of our inmost

self.   We have madly played the guilty game of
Ahaz when he "took down the sea from off the
brasen oxen that were under it, and put it upon a
pavement of stones."

III. We have not lowered the sea! No. *But
we have undone the religious work of the past.*
What skilled and arduous labour did that brazen
sea represent! Consummate artistry it was.   A
world's wonder indeed.   Hiram and his co-workers
had toiled long upon that magnificent laver.   They
had brought all their far-famed genius and industry
to bear upon this sea that was for beauty and for
service in the House of God.   It was a triumph
of Eastern art and a memorial of Eastern toil.
Yet Ahaz and his menials undid it largely if not
absolutely.   Here again he is a type.   "Other
men laboured," says our Lord—and it is well to
take such retrospects.   The men of the religious
past laboured long and severely, with toil of heart
and brain and hands.   "And ye are entered into
their labours," the Apostle adds.   Yes.   Happy
heritage! But how have men often treated that
fair inheritance? Much as Ahaz treated the brasen
sea! We have a faculty for frustrating the labours
into which we have entered.   Oh, it is distressful
how men strive to undo what it has cost so much

to do! What a price our fathers paid, and how they toiled for *liberty of worship*! Yet there are men, religious men, and in no insignificant numbers, who would this very day wipe it out. They labour to undo it. They have succeeded in some lands and in some corners of all lands. Oh, beware of the ecclesiastical Ahaz—he lives and operates among us in Protestant England—who would bring to nothing that "freedom to worship God" which our gallant fathers secured for us at such ineffable price. *Public morality* as we know it to-day is a work of long and laborious achievement. It is a gift of God's grace, but it is the long result of brave and patient human effort. And there are men who would make all that work of none effect. Some avowedly and more with prudent hesitation desire to see the moral restraints of the age cast away. They would obliterate the safeguards of virtue.

Even *the Christian Church*, built up through centuries by such wise master-builders amid stormful oppositions, is not free from those who would undo it. Unhappily there are those who would degrade it into a club: who would reduce to an ethical society: who would make it a meeting-place for merry-makers: who would prostitute it into a political organization. God grant we may,

in the power of the Holy Spirit, be enabled to
drive off the nineteenth-century Ahaz, who
would frustrate the grace of God and efface the
triumphs of religious history.

Have any of us undone the religious work of the
past in our personal character? We are of the
seed-royal. We are of the generation of the godly.
We have had fathers of our flesh who walked with
God. We are of a sacred lineage. How do we
comport ourselves? What legacies of truth and
virtue we have inherited! What have we to show
for it all?

To undo the religious work of the past, in ourselves or in the community, is to cramp the
religious work of the future. To mar our yesterdays may be to blast our to-morrows.

IV. We have not lowered the sea! No. *But
we have treated sacred things irreverently.* Ahaz
laid hands on the brasen sea of the temple as if it
had been a thing of naught. He gave it a short
shrift as if it were a mere " Nehushtan. " A pavement of stone " (R.V.) forsooth was good enough
for God's sacred vessel! And even if we make the
best of it, and read it as some commentators do, " a
pedestal of stone," that does not redeem the gross
irreverence of the deed. For brass he took stones,

and deemed them good enough for the House of God.

You may palliate his irreverence by the plea that he was infected by the ill-example of contemporary kings, but the condonation does not condone. We live in an irreverent age. Without taking account of the contemptuousness of many towards sacred things, how alarming is the decadent reverence of our time. Assuredly we need to sound a reverberating trumpet of alarm in God's holy mountain. Ahaz to-day catches and accentuates the often blatant irreverence of his associates and contemporaries.

Let me plead, especially with younger people, against the grave and growing tendency to an irreverent treatment of sacred entities. Hands off the brasen sea! Shall we treat what God has sanctified as a common thing? Take heed lest we ultimately come to treat the blood of our redemption thus. Remember that golden saying in Cymbeline, "Reverence is the angel of the world." Do not maltreat that radiant angel. Return, O insulted and exiled angel, to the world that is arid, blank, and lustreless if thou be absent from it!

V. We have not lowered the sea! No. *But*

we have sinned through craven fear. Those who
have studied King Ahaz to our profit tell us that
in all probability it was under the shadow of
miserable fear he did this deed of wickedness.
Possibly he "took down the sea from off the
brasen oxen that were under it, and put it
upon a pavement of stones," because he dreaded
the very likely depredations of Tiglath-pileser,
King of Assyria, whose "servant and son" he
was. Possibly he wrought this sacrilege under
the fear of his own straitened circumstances,
and even intended to use the brazen sea and
other furniture of the temple for the purpose
of discharging his obligations to his imperious
creditors.

But, in all likelihood, it was the fear of man
or of circumstances which goaded him to this
depredatory act. And which of us is so clear
of the same evil that we can afford to laugh at
this poor royal poltroon? Fear of man is always
a snare to us. Fear of circumstances sets and
baits many a trap for our souls. "He feared" is
the explanation of many a crime and many a
sin. "Our fears are traitors." Let us fear our
fears and dread our dreads. Many strong men
have fallen thereby. Pray God it may be with
us as with Cromwell and his immortal Ironsides,

who feared God so much that they gradually
grew to fear none else.

VI. We have not lowered the sea! No. Again
let it be freely granted. *But we have preferred
self to God.* The explanation of King Ahaz's
sacrilege which some give us is that he wantonly
robbed God's temple of this splendid sea, in order
to place it in one of his idol-houses, or in order
to make use of it in his palace. Accepting
this explanation, the gravamen of the charge
against Ahaz is that he preferred self to God.
That is the summing-up of it all.

He cared vastly more for his own purposes
than for the purpose of God. So when we come
to analyze this ancient story, it is really very
modern. King Ahaz represents us all. What
man has not sinned as Ahaz sinned? We love
self supremely unless divine grace has changed
our nature. Self supersedes God continually. We
prefer self to God and unmistakably express our
preference. "Self-will is the last enemy to be
subdued," said Madame Guyon. And our self-
knowledge assents to her statement. Is it being
subdued? Are we approximating to its subjugation? Is God becoming all and all to us? Or
is "all of self and none of Thee" the motto of

our atheistic lives? "Unselfishness is the essence of virtue," says Ruskin, that prophet of righteousness. The strength of moral manliness comes of unselfishness. Be not a petty, self-pleasing Ahaz. Be a kingly king. Rule your own spirit. Selfishness is infidelity. Make God your exceeding joy and your exceeding great reward, and self-interest will shrivel and die. To prefer self to God is to elect hell and despise heaven.

VII. We have not lowered the sea! No. Again we accept the resentful repudiation. *But we have caused others to sin.* This, again, King Ahaz did when he "took down the sea from off the brasen oxen that were under it, and put it upon a pavement of stones." He could not and did not accomplish the destructive work alone and unassisted. Ahaz led a priest of God astray. "Urijah the priest "was his trusty henchman. John Trapp describes Urijah as "a fawning parasite to the wicked king," and so he was, but the king was morally responsible for his parasite. Nor was Urijah the only one who was beguiled by Ahaz, for nameless workmen assisted in this most reprehensible proceeding.

"One sinner destroyeth much good." It is bad enough to sin alone, but to associate others in our ill-doing is criminal in degree. There are few sadder epithets in the Bible than that which is repeatedly attached to Jeroboam, "who made Israel to sin." To be a cause of sin in others is to incur unspeakable guilt. Such guilt is being incurred by men continually. How many consciously or unconsciously lead others astray. Our example may make those around us to sin. A spoken word may lure to evil the companions that hear it. We may smile men into sin, and joke them into sin, and sneer them into sin. No warning can be too solemn and urgent against the perpetration of sin. Shall we be the devil's recruiting sergeants? Shall we help to swell the population of hell? God forbid. Let us all be enjoined against being "partakers of other men's sins." Urijah and those who wrought with him were not exculpated because they were led on to sin by King Ahaz. The enticement of sinners does not absolve us from guilt if we consent. When some modern Ahaz shadows your path, cry, being spiritually sensitive, "Lead us not into temptation, but deliver us from evil."

VIII. We have not lowered the sea! Yet once again I concur in your protest. *But we have broken the commandment of God.* God had enjoined

that the brasen sea be fashioned. And more
—God had given commandment that it be placed
on the brasen oxen. Thus and only thus. Thus
and always thus. So that Ahaz distinctly violated
the divine commandment when he removed the
sea from the shoulders of the brasen oxen and
put it on a pavement of stones.

There again we stand in melancholy affinity
with King Ahaz. We, too, have—and that in
more serious ways—broken the commandment of
God. We cannot afford to pose as Pharisees in
presence of this erring king. All our failure and
all our misery springs from our disobedience to God.
Says Mr. Ruskin, in his lovely "Crown of Wild
Olives," "All anarchy is the forerunner of poverty,
and all prosperity begins in obedience." This is
supremely true in the moral and spiritual realm.
Our anarchy of soul explains our poverty of soul.
Our spiritual obedience is the secret of our spiritual
prosperity. Do let us pray that we may realize
this. To hearken to God's commandments is to
have a river-like peace and a righteousness majestic
and beautiful and beneficent as the waves of the
sea. We have need to remember that the
Christian religion is not alone an emotion, nor
an orthodoxy, but a moral obligation. It is not
an æstheticism. It is an obedience.

But some man will say, "I have kept God's commandments from my youth." Have you kept them *all*, my friend? Have you *no* share in the condemnation of King Ahaz? Listen to Paul as he thunders from Mars Hill. His thunders have startled the ages. " He (God) *commandeth* men that they should *all everywhere repent*" (Acts xxvii. 30, R.V.). Have you not broken that commandment? Have you really and finally and for ever changed your mind about your sin and surrendered it? Every impenitent soul is a law-breaker. Hear the aged John, the gentle patriarch of the apostolate on earth. "This is His (God's) *commandment* that we should believe on the name of His Son and love one another" (1 John iii. 23). Have we all obeyed *that* commandment?

God for Christ's sake pardon us. We have all been breakers of His commandments. There is no justification for us in law. There is only justification in the atoning sacrifice of Jesus Christ. Oh, hear and accept that gospel.

So we find that this story of sin is no ancient history. And it matters gravely to us that long ages since "King Ahaz . . . took down the sea from off the brasen oxen that were under it and put it on a pavement of stones."

XVII

THE WISE WOMAN OF ABEL

"A wise woman out of the city."—2 SAM. xx. 16.

WHAT was the name of this woman? We cannot tell, for the Scripture saith not. She is one of the great company of the anonymous people of the Bible. She lived in Abel, a little city in the extreme north of Palestine. Perhaps few are aware that there was a city of this name. We know it as the name of the first martyr, but not as the name of a city. Abel means a meadow, and to this meadow city in the northern highlands of Palestine Joab has come in pursuit of Sheba, the traitor who was a marplot in the kingdom of David, and who had taken refuge in Abel. Joab has besieged Abel and cast up a bank against it. "And all the people that were with Joab battered the wall, to throw it down." It is at this critical moment that the wise woman appears upon the scene, intercedes with Joab, and saves

her city by her wisdom. Let us note some
features of the chieftainess of Abel.

I. SHE WAS REPUTED AS WISE.

If her name is unknown her character is not
unknown. Nameless, she is famous. The historian records her as "a wise woman." That was
her recognized and accepted characterization.
Thus was she known in her city. In ver. 22 we
read, " Then the woman went unto all the people
in her wisdom." Her wisdom was a proverb in
Abel. All the people had tasted of its sovereign
quality. And her fame rings down through the
ages as " a wise woman."

Her fame, in her own time, was intensive rather
than extensive. Abel was but a tiny city, and
though she was well known there yet it was but
a contracted sphere. She lived and moved in a
limited environment. But the quality of reputation is far more than its quantity. You may not
be known far, but you may be known nobly. You
may be famous only in your own house, or street,
or village, but if you are famous for what is true
and beautiful you are famous indeed. The wise
woman of Abel served in a humble sphere, but
she served grandly, and God has taken care her
service shall be honoured and remembered. Her

reputation will live as long as the Book of God shall endure.

It is very curious to notice how freakish even Bible reputations are. What incredibly strange things some Bible people are famous for! One man was famous because he had a bedstead of unusual dimensions. Another was famous for hair of unrivalled length. The freaks of fame! There is a foolish fame. There is an infamous fame. This woman's fame is famous fame.

Why! Because she was famous for wisdom. "A *wise* woman." How many wise women there have been! These terms "woman" and "wise" have often been associated. Well does old Matthew Henry say on this point, "Souls know no difference of sexes; though the man be the head, it does not therefore follow that he has the monopoly of the brains, and therefore he ought not by any salique law to have the monopoly of the crown: many a masculine heart, and more than masculine, has been found in a female breast; nor is the treasure of wisdom the less valuable for being lodged in the weaker vessel."

But even fame for wisdom may not be truly noble fame. There is wisdom and wisdom. There is a wisdom that is foolishness. Some wisdom is branded of God as "earthly, sensual,

devilish." Intelligence and evil may be associated.
An informed mind may be the ally of a base heart.
Educated diabolism is aggravated diabolism.

I think, however, we may say that this wise
woman of Abel was "a wise woman" in the
finest sense. Matthew Henry calls her "a discreet
good woman," and the designation is deserved.
She was a good woman. Read her story and
it is apparent. She loved her city. She cared
for her neighbours. She reverenced Jehovah.
She had genial and gracious qualities adorning
her character. She resented treason and evil-
doing. She had a virile sense of justice. All
this is manifest in her little-read record. Yes.
She was "a wise woman" in the crowning sense
of the epithet.

Let every woman seek to be "a wise woman."
Go among the people of your locality in your
wisdom. Strive for a still higher wisdom than
the woman of Abel knew. Be it yours to attain
to "the wisdom that cometh from above." Would
you know its marks? It is "pure." It is
"peaceable." Wisdom comes to its coronation
when it is pure and peaceable. Oh, let us all be
wise unto salvation. If we lack wisdom let us
ask of God. Why not ask now? Seek by trustful union with Christ the wisdom that is wise

beyond compare. Christ is made of God to all
believers wisdom. We may all be written down
in heaven as wise men and wise women. What
is our reputation in heaven?

II. THIS WISE WOMAN WAS CONSCIOUS OF HAVING GOOD COUNSEL TO GIVE.

When the city of Abel was stormed she in-
tervened. Possibly she was the governor of the
city. But, be that as it may, she spake with
authority in the exigent hour. "Then cried a
wise woman out of the city, Hear, hear; say,
I pray you, unto Joab, Come near hither, that
I may speak with thee" (ver. 16). She utters
herself like a very Deborah. "And when he was
come near unto her, the woman said, Art thou
Joab? And he answered, I am he. Then she
said unto him, Hear the words of thine handmaid.
And he answered, I do hear" (ver. 17). Then
follows her counsel, some elements of which we
shall presently note.

Her counsel was eminently wise. It was
sympathetic with what is right and good. It
was the counsel which the hour needed. Her
injunctions settled the difficulties of the situation.
She had the "Sesame" for the door which seemed
like to be fast-closed for ever.

Well it was that, conscious of being entrusted with such counsel, she cried, "Hear, hear." "Come near hither, that I may speak with thee." "Hear the words of thine handmaid." And well was it for Joab and for the people of Abel that "he answered, I do hear."

God had put a word in this woman's mind and soul, and she knew she had the needed word for the hour. Bishop Hall declares she spoke, "with no less prudence than courage." And the witness is true.

Are you conscious of having good counsel for the world's sins and straits and sorrows? When Joabs lay a siege have you a wise and redeeming word? The wise woman saved her city by her counsel. A poor wise man, Ecclesiastes tells us, saved his city by his wisdom. Such grace to us be given. Have you a word of salvation for the beleaguered people? When Abel is stormed can you speak the word of deliverance? There is a better lore than the wise woman of Abel knew. There is eternal counsel for modern Joabs and modern Abels. I ask myself and you—Have we possessed ourselves of it? Many a misguided Joab awaits our counsel. How long shall he have to wait? Oh, fare forth and tell him the word of God to-day. You may save your city by your word as the wise woman saved her city, and yet more abundantly. Be it ours to speak the needed word. There is no counsel so inclusive, so always pertinent, so far-reaching, so universally apposite as the gospel of Christ. Go forth, ye men and women who are to salvation wise, and cry, " Hear, hear." Away at once, lest Abel be destroyed, and give saving counsel to the people. Cry and spare not. Lift up thy voice like a trumpet. Say, " Hear, and your soul shall live."

III. THE WISE WOMAN OF ABEL APPRE-CIATED NOBLE HISTORY.

What a powerful plea is her appeal to the historical quality of the city of Abel. She plies Joab with this, and it has much argumentative significance: " They were wont to speak in old time, saying, They shall surely ask counsel at Abel : and so they ended the matter" (ver. 18). Her argument is that a city with such a history is a city no marauder should destroy.

This woman was wise, in this as in much else, that she was a student of history. She was conversant with the records of the past. She knew the times that had gone over Abel. She had acquaintance with the beneficent *rôle* her people had played, who now slept in the dust of the earth.

It is well to know all we may of "old time"; especially all that was wise, honourable and philanthropic in "old time." I commend the wise woman of Abel to you as an example in this particular.

She was familiar with great historical utterances. "They were wont to speak in old time, saying." She knew the proverbs of the ancients. It is good, every way good, to know the sayings of history. We are too careless of what "they were wont to speak in old time." Words of vanished people should be treasured words. If they of old time are gone, many of their words are preserved to us. Do we know them? Do we trouble to read them? How vain is the vanity which deems itself too wise for the utterances of the old time!

History is a Bible inspired of God and profitable. The hand of God in history should never be unrevealed to us. Read the history of nations. Read the history of Britain. Read Church history. Read the history of your own special Church. All history is theological if we read it aright. Time is ever ablaze with God.

I would especially urge young people to emulate the wise woman of Abel in her knowledge of

the utterances of history. " They were wont to
speak in old time." Modern times have no
monopoly of words of wisdom. Search ancient
literature. Read and re-read the old divines.
Let the ancient voices sound in your soul, and
that soul shall abound in music. Especially read
your Bible. Oh, be not negligent of this ancient
literature. Hear the voices of the prophets and
of the Apostles. " Holy men spake as they
were moved of God." Shall they speak in vain
to us ? God forbid. Value all noble historic
records, but with greatest estimation value the
revelations of God to His ancient servants. They
are still applicable and still powerful. " They
were wont to speak in old time," and their words
are recorded for us on whom the ends of the
ages are fallen.

IV. THIS WISE WOMAN PRIZED PROVED
CENTRES OF KNOWLEDGE.

She protested against Abel being destroyed by
Joab, and this is one of the grounds of her protest :
" They were wont to speak in old time, saying,
They shall surely ask counsel at Abel : and so they
ended the matter " (ver. 18).

Abel as a centre of light had been tried repeatedly of old, and it had never failed. The

little city of the far north had been a highland
oracle : a shrine of knowledge.   When people were
perplexed, baffled, sore pressed with enmity, their
advisers said, "They shall surely ask counsel at
Abel." The people of Abel had been always a wise
people.   The city was famous for its trusted
counsellors.   So famous was it that its counsel was
deemed final.   " And so they ended the matter."
Abel's word was absolute. When Abel spoke its
word was the last word on any subject. Abel
had long been approved as a central point of
luminosity.

And shall such a centre be destroyed? No!
cries the wise woman.   She was proud of Abel's
history.   She gloried in the fair fame of the city
She holds right dear what had long been an
instrument of enlightenment.   A place where
counsel " ended the matter " through long tracts
of time may well be dearly prized. Abel means
" meadows." Let meadows that were a delight
to generations gone be sacredly preserved by
succeeding generations.

There are Abels to-day of which "they were wont
to speak in old time saying, They shall surely ask
counsel at Abel: and so they ended the matter."
There are *places* that have long been proved as
centres of knowledge.   Inevitably the old people

sought counsel there.   Whatever difficulty arose, it
it was taken for granted these centres would be
appealed to : " They shall *surely* ask counsel at
Abel." There are *institutions* that have met the
deepest needs of centuries. Counsel was asked
of them, "and so they ended the matter."   There
are *books* which have yielded similar proof of their
power to counsel. Such a Book is the Bible. It
is an Abel. Of this literary city, " they were wont
to speak in old time saying, Thou shalt surely ask
counsel at Abel : and so they ended the matter."
Do you prize such places, such institutions, such
books?   Is the wisdom of the ages precious to
you ? When these things are assailed by some
vandalic Joab do you resent the assault and defend
the assaulted ?

Many proved centres of blessing are attacked
to day. Long-proved Abels are tested with remorseless testing. Joabs and their confederates
are battering the venerable walls to throw them
down. Oh, stand up for Abel! Realize how it
has met the wants of the ages. Be loyal to that
which gave your fathers light and salvation.

V. The Wise Woman of Abel was Conscious of Uprightness.

What a fine apologia of her character she uttered

to Joab! She said, " I am one of them that are peaceable and faithful in Israel" (ver. 19). She must have had a lovely mind. She evidently had a choice vocabulary. Some of the grandest oracles of the Bible were uttered by women. There are no serener pearls than have fallen from feminine caskets. And here is a notable specimen : " I am one of them that are peaceable and faithful in Israel."

She claims that there were many such in Abel. The epithets are plural in the original, say our scholars. " I am *one of them* that are peaceable and faithful." Only one of a goodly company.

She is obliged to admit, however, that *all* in Israel were not of this choice order. Perhaps the peaceable and faithful were not predominant in Abel. Have they ever been predominant any-where ? When the majority of mankind are graced with such great attributes there will surely be new heavens and a new earth.

Ponder the goodly epithets of this goodly woman. " Peaceable" she was. She was possessed of peace. She had a quiet heart—God's best gift to men and women. The dove of heaven had descended and abode upon her. All around her was unrest. A traitor lurked in her city. Death gloomed the horizon, for Joab was thundering at Abel's walls.

Yet was this great soul "peaceable." Oh to be sharers in her calm even when sharers in her outward disquietude. I may live in assaulted Abel and yet may be peaceable. The wise woman claimed that she strongly desired peace with everyone, for that also is the force of this word " peaceable." About her were some who were inimical to the king and the kingdom. Anarchy was represented in all its hideous features ; even in Abel, Sheba shadowed the city with his hateful presence. But this valiant woman is " peaceable." She is loyal to the monarchy. She has no grudge against any. She regards none as foes. Bloodshed is remote from her thought and utterly repugnant to her desire.

Peaceable people are the goodliest of a nation's assets. How precious are they wherever they are found ! As citizens as neighbours, as Church members, they are of highest worth. Cultivate that disposition. It is godly and will work godliness. Righteousness effects peaceableness. It is the very bloom of character.

The consciousness of such qualities is a precious possession. The wise woman is to be coveted in that she could say, " I am one of them that are peaceable and faithful in Israel." Christians will cherish this consciousness, gratefully adoring the saving grace by which it is imparted. They will in

nowise ascribe it to themselves that they are
" peaceable and faithful." The indwelling Christ
alone will they glorify. If you can revert to your
character with any degree of satisfaction, give
God the glory. And gratefully prize such grace-
given consciousness. To know that we possess
the durable riches of character is to have matter
of eternal song.

VI. THIS NOBLE WOMAN LIVED FOR
OTHERS.

She described herself, whilst remonstrating with
Joab, as " a mother in Israel " (ver. 19).

It appears to me that this is distinctly a
reference to herself, and not to her city. To
speak of a city as a mother in Israel is unheard
of. When earlier in Scripture the phrase is used,
it refers to a person, and not to a place. To
use it of a city is to give it a very forced and
unlikely application. No. The wise woman tells
Joab that in seeking to destroy a city he is
also seeking to destroy herself, " a mother in
Israel."

I do not know what the men of Abel were
nor where they were at this critical moment that
a woman must needs mediate for the city. But
if the men' were a little brood, there was one

woman at least who compensated for them all.
" A mother in Israel." She delighted to live for
Israel. Her days were filled with motherly service.
She had a mother's heart towards the people.

What we all owe to the motherly women of
the world and of the Church! Deborah sang
of herself as " a mother in Israel," and though
an iron mother, she was a true mother. This
wise woman of Abel was a strong yet tender
mother. Paul speaks of the mother of Rufus as
" his mother and mine." Such women are everyone's mothers. Israel would be lonesome, and
cold, and sad without such loving and helpful
souls. We owe a special obligation to the " aged
women " who have been mothers in Israel. They
have been centres of unspeakable blessing. They
have made for the peace of the Church. They have
turned the Church into a home. The noble service
of women which the Son of Mary has inspired
is not the least of His triumphs.

Let every woman who has learned Christ seek
to be a mother or a sister in Israel. Let them
not spend their lives on miserable ends. Let
them not live for themselves. Well will they do
to copy the example of this mother in Israel,
who delighted to give herself for others in the
ancient city of Abel. All alike, men and women,

may well blush that they have not more constantly lived for others. There are many ways
of being mothers and fathers, brothers and sisters
in Israel. Israel needs all kinds of service. All
our talents may find ample scope in seeking the
good of Israel. For what are we living? Who
is better for our dwelling here? Beware lest in
these self-pleasing days we fail of honest service
for Israel and stand condemned at the judgment.
Beware lest the wise woman of Abel shall
condemn us in that awful day because she was
a mother in Israel, and we, with privileges greater
far than hers, lived only for ourselves. Lose
your life for Christ's sake, and for evermore you
shall find it again with joy beyond all telling.

VII. THE WISE WOMAN DEPRECATED THE DESTRUCTION OF GOD'S INHERITANCE.

"Why wilt thou swallow up the inheritance
of the Lord?" (ver. 19) she cries in sorrow and
anger. As Poole puts it, "She doth modestly
reprove Joab." That is a fine conception of a
city, "the inheritance of the Lord." And the
wise woman is in noble fellowship in uttering
such a sentiment. David described the kingdom
as "the inheritance of the Lord." The Psalms
speak of the people of Israel as God's inheritance.

But Paul carries the idea to its glorious climax
when he dilates on "the riches of the glory of
His inheritance in the saints." A city, a kingdom,
a nation, the Christian Church are alike pourtrayed
as "the inheritance of the Lord." It is a grand
and inspiring idea. Every city is God's inheritance. All peoples are God's inheritance.
Christian believers are peculiarly the inheritance
of the Lord.

Let this question be addressed to all who would
destroy cities and peoples. "Why wilt thou
swallow up the inheritance of the Lord?" All
places and all peoples acquire a new dignity and
sacredness when they are regarded as God's
inheritance. All life is invested with sanctity
when so regarded. Beware of swallowing up
God's inheritance! If all things are of God,
then to hurt and destroy is sacrilege.

Especially may the wise woman's query give
pause to the Joabs who are too willing to swallow
up the Church of Christ. Her "why" may well
pierce and penetrate their souls. God's people
are God's inheritance. Those who would destroy
such a people are robbers of the worst species,
for they rob God. Stay thy hand, O latter-day
Joab. God delights in His believing people with
supreme delight. His inheritance in them has

"riches" and "glory" in His estimation. "Why wilt thou swallow up the inheritance of the Lord?" Would the world be better for such destruction? God's inheritance is the world's sanative element, and its guarantee of preservation. Joab disclaimed such a purpose as the wise woman attributed to him. Happy is the man who can utter such a disclaimer. More happy still is he who delights in God's inheritance, who loves to help it, who prizes it beyond compare.

Oh, be loyal to the inheritance of the Lord! Deprecate its destruction. There are many forces adverse to it in these days. Full many would rejoice if they could swallow it up quick. Plead with such. Protest against such. Shall God have a poor inheritance? God forbid. By prayer and every form of service possible to us let us avert the wreckage of the inheritance of the Lord.

VIII. THIS WISE WOMAN OF ABEL USED HER INFLUENCE WELL.

Herein she is again an ensample to us all. Influence is one of the subtlest and most effective attributes of mankind. It may be an incalculable good or an ineffable evil. How admirably the wise woman traded with this precious talent! With Joab she exercised her influence most

skilfully and beneficently. She proposed terms,
just and reasonable, in which Joab immediately
acquiesced. Joab had explained to her that Sheba,
the traitor, was hiding in the city; if he were
delivered over, Joab and his forces would depart
from the city. Said the severely just arbitress,
" Behold, his head shall be thrown to thee over
the wall " (ver. 21). She was as good as her word,
and the besieging forces were immediately with-
drawn, and the city of Abel was left in peace.
The sequel reflects credit alike upon the wise
woman and on the compliant Joab.

This mother in Israel used her rare influence
with the people of Abel in equally felicitous
fashion. " Then the woman went unto all the
people in her wisdom " (ver. 22). She proclaimed
to the citizens of the beleaguered city what she
had proposed to the beleaguering chief, and they
unanimously assented.

Further, she used her great influence for the
suppression of evil. She secured a righteous,
a sternly righteous, retribution upon the traitor.
The decapitated Sheba was a witness to her
influence in behalf of justice. The traitor's trunk
attested her loathing of wrong and her passion
for the right.

And finally, her influence effected the salvation

of her city. When Sheba's head was cast over the walls of Abel to Joab, "he blew a trumpet, and they retired from the city, every man to his tent. And Joab returned to Jerusalem unto the king." So the wise woman stands out on history's page as the deliverer of her city.

All this is an impressive illustration of the right use of personal influence. God has dowered us with the precarious gift of influence. Each man and woman tells for good or evil on some others. Does our influence make for blessedness? How do we reason with the Joab whose ear we gain? Do we lead him to happy or fateful goals? What is our influence on the community around us? How do we ply the people of Abel? Does our influence make against evil? Are we, in however humble a degree, working for the salvation of the place we dwell in? These are vital and pregnant questions. Be it ours to use them as candles with which to search our hearts. Well will it be with us if we with our Christian illumination use our influence as faithfully as the wise woman did hers in the city of Abel in ancient times. Her influence was that of "wisdom," but it was a very limited "wisdom" when compared with Christian wisdom. With nobler instrumentalities we may, through grace, effect infinitely nobler results. We may save with spiritual salvation the cities we dwell in.

Bishop Hall, in his invaluable " Contemplations," forcefully applies the salvation of Abel. "Spiritually the case is ours. Every man's breast is a city enclosed. Every sin is a traitor that lurks within those walls. God calls to us for Sheba's head ; neither hath He any quarrel to our person, but for our sin. If we love the head of our traitor above the life of our soul we shall justly perish in the vengeance. We cannot be more willing to part with our sin than our merciful God is to withdraw His judgments."

O city of Mansoul, throw out the traitor's head ! Give no foothold to Sheba ! O city of Mansoul, open wide thy gates to Emmanuel the Son of Shaddai !

XVIII

AN IDYLL OF THE FLOOD

" And the dove came in to him in the evening ; and, lo, in her mouth was an olive leaf."—GEN. viii. 11.

I. HERE IS A SUCCESSFUL QUEST AFTER FAILURE.

A S the flood was subsiding, Noah made repeated quests concerning the habitableness of the earth. He sent forth a raven, but the dark and restless messenger brought him no satisfaction. He sent forth a dove, but the bird of peace carried him no message of peace. Twice Noah's quest is doomed to failure. But once again he sends forth the dove from the window of the ark. And this time the quest is crowned with solace and success. "The dove came in to him in the evening ; and, lo, in her mouth was an olive leaf."

How frequently life's eager quests fail ! Alike in things temporal and in things spiritual is this so. We send forth our raven—and the quest is a disappointment. We commission our dove, and the dispiriting history repeats itself. Failure darkens the day and deepens the gloom of the night. Verily Noah and his pathetic quests parabolize us and our quests, always pathetic, often tragic.

But I bid you hope! After failure and repeated failure comes success. "And the dove came in to him in the evening ; and, lo, in her mouth was an olive leaf." In so far as any quest of ours has failed, we do well to examine into *the reason* of the failure. Why have raven and dove alike proved abortive messengers ? To know the secret of failure is to know the secret of success. One of George Meredith's vigorous characters "had never failed in an undertaking without stripping bare to expose to himself where he had been wanting in intention and determination." An admirable example! We shall turn failures into triumphs if we frankly criticize our failures.

Do not let us lose heart and hope though earnest quests have failed. If Noah's first messenger bring no message, let him send forth a second ; and if that, too, carry no tidings, let him open the window of the ark and commission a third. We lose everything in life when we lose heart. Hope is the salt of our days. It is said that Sir Walter Raleigh wrote with a diamond on a window-pane :

> Fain would I climb but that I fear to fall.

Witty Queen Elizabeth passing presently saw the words and wrote beneath :

> If thine heart fail thee, do not climb at all.

All life's climbings depend upon the heart with which we engage upon them. Better never climb than climb with a fearful heart. Let not our quests cease because up to now they have failed. "Put a cheerful courage on." Send forth the dove again, O disappointed Noah! Be stout-hearted and hopeful amid reiterated failure. At evening, mayhap, the dove may return with an olive leaf in her mouth.

Do not relax effort because of failure. Noah fails but tries again. He fails again, and again he sends forth his dove. So do we. Sit not down in your ark dismayed and dejected because your endeavours have failed. You will bring a curse upon yourself if you give up your attempts. Admirable ever is the child's maxim: "If at first you don't succeed, try, try again."

Above all do not dismiss a good agency even if it has not yielded what you hoped. There are Noahs who slay their dove if it bring not at once the desired message. Others there be who scornfully consign the dove to banishment. It is a foolish policy, whether in things temporal or spiritual. Because an agency has failed once, nay twice, it does not follow that it shall fail perpetually. The dove's flight may be abortive the first time and delightfully successful afterwards.

Have you sought the evangelical salvation and failed to find it? Do not surrender your attempt. Often is God found after many an intermediate failure. The dreary reminiscence, " I sought Him, but I found Him not," may be erewhile lost in the rapturous memory, " I found Him whom my soul loveth."

Has prayer yielded you little or no conscious benefit? Oh, do not dismiss that mighty force. Give it protracted trial. Failure shall pave the way to success. Unanswered prayers prepare us to receive answers in God's good time. With long patience pray and pray again, and or ever you are aware the God-sent olive leaf shall make you glad.

Has Bible-study afforded you little profit? And do you contemplate closing your Bible to open it no more? I beg you relegate not that

Book of Books to the shelf where stands the unread literature. Search it once again. Cry yet more earnestly to the living oracles, nor shall they long be dumb to thine appeal. Though God's word seem unresponsive, yet if thou makest repeated appeal it shall satisfy thy longings.

Have you wrought hard in Christian work and seen nothing but failure? Surrender not your task. Ply it diligently though under lowering skies. "Thou knowest not which shall prosper, whether this or that." Nor knowest thou when it shall prosper. Many a loving quest may fail, yet success shall ultimately fill your soul with jubilee.

Let all discouraged ones take heart. Hope on when all seems hopeless. Noah and his quests are not forgotten of God. God watches when He seems not to watch. "Hope thou in God." says this idyll of the flood.

II. Behold Comfort amid Shadows.

It was "in the evening" the dove brought its halcyon message to Noah. "At eventide" (R.V.) he was reassured and gladdened. It was doubly "eventide" to the patriarch. Not only were the natural shadows falling, but shadows deeper and darker enfolded his spirit. Who can tell what

he suffered whilst he voyaged amid those
sweltering floods? Memories, fears, overwhelming
emotions—these made "eventide" in his obedient
and believing soul. It is a parable. God's bird
often comes to us amid the shadows. "At even-
time" the olive leaf is ours. Life is replete with
shadows. The most shining river is erewhile
darkened with strange shadows. Which of us
has lived a quite unshadowed life? I have seen
shadows photographed. But never have I seen
the sorrow-shadows adequately portrayed. Who
can photograph a grief? Only experience can
realize the deep shadows which fall on the children
of men.

But God gives us comfort amid shadows. He
sends us His dove "at eventide." We need never
know the shades of evening without heaven's
dove. Is this not a parable of how the Holy
Spirit comes when the shadows gather? The
Spirit descends "like a dove," as on the Christ,
so on the Christian. The dove is a lovely emblem
of the Holy Spirit. The dove is in the Old Testament the sacrificial bird, the bird that brings
atonement. And how powerfully amid life's
shadows the Spirit of God applies to us the atonement of the Saviour. Nothing comforts in life's
doubts and sorrows and fears like the messenger

of atonement.   To realize amid my shadowed
hours that Christ's atoning sacrifice avails abundantly for me—this is the strongest consolation of
my sorrows.   Do you know this blessedness?
Does the Spirit " like a dove " wing its ray to you
" at eventide " with a message of pardon through
the offering once offered?   Then truly you have
comfort amid the shadows.   The dove is always
the symbol of purity.   And how often amid life's
menacing shadows the Spirit of God brings us
purifying influences.   " Like a dove " He comes
and bears to us hallowing and cleansing.   Was it
not amid the shadows the Spirit cleansed your
soul?   It is not seldom the hour of darkness that
is the hour of purification.   If the Dove holy and
divine bring us purity amid our darkening experiences, we shall have what Baxter calls "vigorous
real comfort."

Let me apply this parable in another direction.
We shall have comfort amid the shadows if we
have ourselves a dove-like spirit.   This is how
Matthew Henry applies my text: " The olive
branch, which was an emblem of peace, was brought,
not by the raven, the bird of prey, nor by a gay
and proud peacock, but by a mild, patient, humble
dove.   It is a dove-like disposition that brings into
the soul earnests of rest and joy."

Are we cherishing that " dove-like disposition "? if so, when life's "eventide" settles on us we shall have " earnests of rest and joy." Oh, put out thine hand for that dove. Receive what God waits to give, a disposition of tenderness, meekness, patience, love. Sure as this is thine thou shalt have the olive leaf when evening shades prevail.

What of the shadows, if we have the dove and its sweet message! What of its being "toward eventide," if Christ be constrained to abide with us! What of the nightfall, if God has given us " the morning star "! They shall not lack comfort amid the shadows who receive the dove with its olive leaf.

III. My text is an illustration of A SLIGHT MESSENGER WITH A GREAT MESSAGE.

God uses many and varied messengers. He has apostles in infinite variety. In the case before us God guided a bird for Noah's instruction and encouragement. This little homely bird was, as Keil puts it, "a herald of salvation."

In our common life we often witness messengers who seem incongruous with their momentous message. The telegraph wire is a slender messenger, but what tremendous messages it carries. Who could have thought such messages could come by such a medium! A pigeon carries epoch-marking messages alike across battlefields and plains of peace. How inadequate appears the messenger for such messages! A cheque or a postal order are slight messengers, yet are they welcomed for the messages they bear. The Bible abounds in such illustrations, for God loves to bring weak things to great issues. Elijah is fed daily and abundantly by ravens. The lad's loaves satisfy the hunger of the multitude when Christ so ordains. A fish flitting along the waters carries the coin which pays the master's tribute. A dove, the lowly, quiet, domestic bird, brings Noah the message of a new world. Oh the grace of God who uses slight messengers to annunciate thrilling tidings!

Then let us think more of the message than of the messenger. Some of us are so occupied with criticism of the messenger that we miss the message. The herald of salvation may be lowly, but it is the salvation, not the herald, we must consider. The preacher may be ineloquent, but his message has an eloquence all its own. The teacher may utter his lesson poorly, but to receive the lesson may be regeneration. Take care lest in depreciating the dove you lose the olive leaf!

Do not, I pray you, despise minute and in-

significant media. They perchance bring God's
message to us. Doves may carry revelations.
"Who hath despised the day of small things?"
The day of small things is a divinely-created day.
Be ever on the look-out for divine messages.
Care not by what messengers they come. But
be solicitous that they come. Agonize to receive
them. Say, "Speak, Lord, for Thy servant
heareth." Be on the *qui vive* for a fresh olive leaf.
It is the listeners who hear God's word. It is
the watchers who perceive the returning dove. It
is they who put out their hand who receive the
"sweet messenger of rest." Be ours the high
grace of being daily recipients of messages from
heaven.

IV. This idyll presents us with A SLENDER
SIGN OF GREAT SIGNIFICATION.

When the dove came in to Noah in the evening
"lo," exclaims the lovely story, "in her mouth
was an olive leaf." No wonder the historian cries
"lo"! Well might he be astonished and seek
to awaken our astonishment. Noah was awaiting
a sign. And when the sign appears how altogether
slender, how all but trivial it seems. "Lo, in
her mouth was an olive leaf." The margin of
the Revised Version describes it "as a fresh olive

leaf." Yet, if slender, the sign was interesting, not to say poetic. God's signs are always lovely. God's signs are ever instinct with poetry. This is the first mention of the olive in Scripture. But from this time no tree is more often found among the arboreous allusions of the Bible. This reference to the olive is the earliest instance of a tree being named in these records. Always the olive is the great symbol of peace and of prosperity.

When Noah perceived the " fresh olive leaf " we are told that, " *So* Noah knew that the waters were abated from off the earth." How much that " so " portends ! The olive leaf—that slender sign—had vast and far-reaching signification. It pointed to a renovated world. That fragile sign indicated vistas of meaning all but immeasurable.

Signs are often insignificant in themselves. It is their signification which makes them great. A wedding-ring, especially one long worn, is slim. But what does it signify? Love that has stood triumphantly the storms of life. Union that no shock could sever. That wedding-ring points to long years of changeful experience. It hints at elysian joys and purgatorial fires. Who could write the story of which that ring is the insignificant sign? I see a slight blue ribbon on yon man's coat. Of what is it a sign? Of a noble renunciation.   Perhaps of a fierce battle grandly won.   Next to nothing is that blue ribbon in itself, but it may mean that through grace divine a man has got the drink-devil under his triumphant feet.

The blind of yonder window is drawn!   A slight sign that drawn blind!   Yes.   But of what does it speak with tragic eloquence?   Of death victorious.   Of love heart-broken.   Of a spirit gone to God who gave it.

The sacraments are slender signs.   The sprinkled water drops.   The broken bread.   The chalice and its wine.   Yet who can gauge their evangelical and mystical meaning?   To faith that water is the baptism of the cleansing Spirit of God.   To faith that broken bread becomes " My body," and that wine "My blood."

Wise and blessed are they who study the signification of common things and see the gospel of signs.   Happy they who can read the meaning of the olive leaf.

What was the signification of the fresh olive leaf to Noah?

That leaf was an illustration of the sacramental quality of Nature.   It was Nature speaking of God.   It was a gospel in a leaf.   There is a gospel in every leaf if we had but senses to discern it. The fresh olive leaf told Noah of God's working in the world. He had been working destructively : now His deed is redemptive. The waters are abating! Retribution is exacted. Mercy is once again rejoicing against judgment.

Do we read all Nature as sacramental? Do we see a theology in a leaf? Does Nature expound God to us? " To thoughtful observators," says Sir Thomas Browne in his " Christian Morals," "the whole world is a phylactery." Ah, verily it is ! The cosmos is writ large with the revelatory texts of God.

The olive leaf signified that sorrow was vanishing fast. The declivities of the hills are clear. The dove has found dry and clean places, for on no other will it rest. The waters are abating. How often God by small signs tells His troubled children of the approaching end of their sorrow ! We, too, have received our fresh olive leaf, and have known that the proud waters of our tribulation were passing away. Praised be God for the consolatory import of a slender sign.

The olive leaf received at the window of the ark meant that sin had been destroyed. The rampant iniquity of the world had been completely effaced. By signs slight in themselves does God sometimes assure His children that sin no longer has dominion in the cosmos of their soul. Are you looking for such a sign?

The olive leaf was a beauteous sign of God's gift of peace. Doubly was Noah assured of peace, for the dove is the bird of peace even as the olive is the tree of peace. The God of peace had not forgotten His much-tried servant. " Peace, perfect peace," was the sweet experience of which the olive leaf is symbol. What signs of peace God sends His people! By many a sign, often slight in itself, we know that our God is " the very God of peace."

The olive leaf was a sign of abundant hope. Oh, Noah, the best is yet to be! Death is overborne by life. The radiant future prints its kiss upon Noah's wrinkled brow. His yesterday was dark, but his to-morrow shall be glorious. The God of hope speaks His glad gospel of hope by means of an olive leaf.

Let us study the slightest signs of God and His messages. Be quick to interpret the supernatural in nature. Discern the gospels that hide in common things. As Smetham nobly says, " It is the man who knows nothing common or unclean that wrings the fine essences out of Nature." Be you and I that man!

V. Is not this idyllic scene A PATHETIC PARABLE OF SALVATION?

How often, "like Noah's dove," we "flit between rough seas and stormy skies!" Have we no Noah to fly to? Noah means "Rest." Who is our Rest, our redeeming Noah? "Jesus, who delivered us from the wrath to come." O soul of man, return unto thy Rest! Fly, by simple faith, to the outstretched hand of the heavenly Noah.

And is not Christ our ark of safety? You *have* "wings like a dove," oh, fly to the ark! There is no other refuge for these guilty, storm-tossed souls of ours. Bishop Hall quaintly says, "The dove was a true citizen of the ark." May each of us be "a true citizen of the ark"!